Comparing and Ordering Positive and Negative Numbers

You can use a number line to compare positive and negative numbers. The numbers on a number line get larger as you move to the right and smaller as you move to the left.

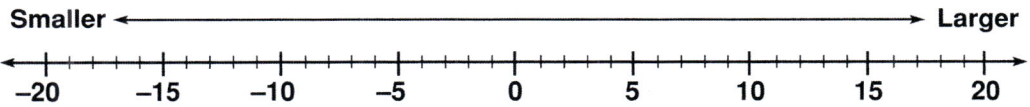

Compare −3 to −4.

> Find each number on the number line.
>
> −3 is to the right of −4, so −3 is greater than −4.
>
> −3 > −4

Compare −15 to 5.

> Find each number on the number line.
>
> −15 is to the left of 5, so −15 is less than 5.
>
> −15 < 5

Compare each set of numbers. Write > or <.

1. −2 < 3   4 ☐ −3   0 ☐ 2   −6 ☐ −5   12 ☐ −12
2. −5 ☐ −10   1 ☐ −2   −15 ☐ 5   −19 ☐ 9   10 ☐ 3
3. 17 ☐ 12   −8 ☐ −7   −6 ☐ 0   14 ☐ −13   7 ☐ −7
4. −3 ☐ 2   16 ☐ 12   −4 ☐ 4   −8 ☐ −9   −11 ☐ 10
5. −14 ☐ −15   −20 ☐ −16   −17 ☐ 17   −1 ☐ −2   3 ☐ 0
6. 5 ☐ −10   6 ☐ 8   −12 ☐ 10   15 ☐ −1   19 ☐ −19
7. −10 ☐ −4   8 ☐ −8   −7 ☐ 6   3 ☐ 1   −16 ☐ −13
8. 11 ☐ 12   20 ☐ −16   −18 ☐ −17   13 ☐ 0   −20 ☐ −5

Write each set of numbers in order from smallest to largest.

9. −10, 3, 0   7, 9, −7   −4, 2, −12   −6, −15, −8
   −10, 0, 3
10. 15, 8, 0   16, −11, −2   14, −20, 5   −1, 2, 0
11. −16, −13, −18   6, 20, −14   1, −2, −3   −5, −8, 9

Solve.

12. Which is colder: −12° or −20°?

    Answer_____

13. Which is higher: −3,000 feet or 3,000 feet?

    Answer_____

14. Which is warmer: −30° or 3°?

    Answer_____

15. Which is lower: −500 feet or −1,000 feet?

    Answer_____

Powers and Square Roots

A number multiplied by itself, such as 4 × 4, can be written as 4^2. We read 4^2 as 4 to the second power or 4 squared. 4 × 4 × 4 is 4^3 or 4 to the third power or 4 cubed.

$4^2 = 4 \times 4 = 16$
$4^3 = 4 \times 4 \times 4 = 64$

Finding the root of a number is the opposite of finding a power. When you find the square root of 16, or $\sqrt{16}$, ask yourself *what number multiplied times itself equals 16?*

$\sqrt{16} = 4$ because $4 \times 4 = 16$

Find 5^2

$5^2 = 5 \times 5$
$5^2 = 25$

Find 7^3

$7^3 = 7 \times 7 \times 7$
$7^3 = 49 \quad \times 7$
$7^3 = 343$

Find $\sqrt{81}$

$9 \times 9 = 81$
$\sqrt{81} = 9$

Find each answer.

1. 3^2 $\sqrt{64}$ 4^3 7^2 $\sqrt{4}$
   $3 \times 3 = 9$ $8 \times 8 = 64$
               $\sqrt{64} = 8$

2. $\sqrt{100}$ 9^3 6^3 14^2 12^2

3. 8^3 $\sqrt{36}$ 5^2 $\sqrt{16}$ 1^2

4. 10^3 $\sqrt{144}$ 16^3 5^3 6^2

5. $\sqrt{169}$ 8^2 2^3 9^2 $\sqrt{121}$

6. $\sqrt{25}$ 20^2 0^2 4^2 $\sqrt{49}$

Solve.

7. Aaron built a deck that measures 16 feet on each side. What is the area of the deck? (Use the formula for area of a square, $A = s^2$.)

   Answer _____

8. Sheila built her children a toy box that measures 2 feet by 2 feet by 2 feet. What is the volume of the box? (Use the formula for the volume of a cube, $V = s^3$.)

   Answer _____

STECK-VAUGHN
Mathematics Skill Book
Algebra

Contents

Positive and Negative Numbers	2–3
Powers and Square Roots	4
Numerical and Algebraic Expressions	5–10
Solving Simple Equations	11–12
Checking Up	13
Adding and Subtracting Signed Numbers	14–16
Addition and Subtraction Equations	17–18
Checking Up	19
Multiplying and Dividing Signed Numbers	20–21
Adding, Subtracting, Multiplying, and Dividing Signed Numbers	22
Multiplication and Division Equations	23–24
Checking Up	25
Solving Fraction and Two-Step Equations	26–28
Checking Up	29
Using Formulas for Distance, Interest, and Cost	30–33
Using Geometric Formulas	34–37
Ratios, Proportions, and Similar Triangles	38–40
Checking Up	41
Graphing an Equation	42
Slope of a Line	43
Progress Review	44–45
Answer Key	46–48

Introduction

Algebra Mathematics Skill Book is designed to enable you to work on your own toward mastery of algebraic expressions and simple equations as well as the fundamentals of geometric formulas. The pages in this book combine the advantages of a textbook and a workbook by first showing you how certain types of problems should be solved and then providing similar practice exercises.

Mastery of the concepts presented in *Algebra Mathematics Skill Book* is aided by clear explanations and numerous examples. You should not treat some of the skill pages, especially those at the beginning of each content area, as being too elementary. These skills must be mastered before you can move on to more advanced exercises.

You can use the answers provided on pages 46–48 to check your own work. You should correct any errors before beginning work on the next skill page. Use the progress test on pages 44–45 to find out how well you have mastered the concepts in this book.

Copyright by Aztec Software, LLC.

All rights reserved. No part of this work may be reproduced or transmitted in any form or by any means, electronic or mechanical, including photocopying or recording, or by any information storage or retrieval system, without the prior written permission of the copyright owner, unless such copying is expressly permitted by federal copyright law. Requests for permission to make copies of any part of the work should be addressed to permissions@aztecsoftware.com or Aztec Software, LLC, 51 Commerce Street, Springfield, NJ, 07081.

ISBN 978-1-954456-32-7

1 2 3 4 5 6 7 8 9 10   PX2050   30 29 28 27 26 25 24 23 22 21

Positive and Negative Numbers

A number line shows the order of positive and negative numbers. Positive numbers are to the right of zero. Negative numbers are to the left of zero.

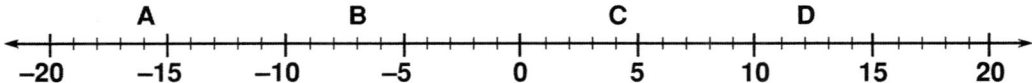

Find the letter that corresponds to –16.

> Find zero on the number line. Count 16 marks to the left.
>
> The letter at –16 is A.

Find the number that corresponds to C.

> Find C above the number line. Count the number of marks to the right from zero to C.
>
> The number at C is 4.

Use the number line below to find the letter that corresponds to each number.

1. –19 __A__   0 ____   –2 ____   8 ____   20 ____

2. –6 ____   3 ____   10 ____   18 ____   –12 ____

3. 5 ____   13 ____   –16 ____   15 ____   –10 ____

Use the number line below to find the number that corresponds to each letter.

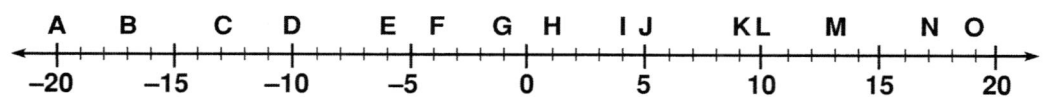

4. C __–13__   H ____   J ____   A ____   D ____

5. O ____   M ____   I ____   G ____   B ____

6. K ____   N ____   L ____   F ____   E ____

Write each expression as either a positive or negative number.

7. 5 to the right of 0
   5

   7 to the left of 0

   2 to the right of –2

8. 3 to the left of 7

   4 to the right of –10

   10 to the left of 20

9. 9 to the right of –5

   6 to the left of 1

   11 to the right of –8

10. 4 to the left of 4

    2 to the right of –1

    8 to the left of –3

Evaluating Numerical Expressions

A numerical expression is a group of numbers and math operations such as 3 + 4 or (3 + 8) · 5 (the sum of 3 plus 8 multiplied by 5). When an expression has more than one operation, you must do the operations in a specific order to evaluate, or find the answer of, the expression. The rules below show the order in which math operations must be done.

Order of Operations

1. **Do operations within parentheses.**
2. **Do operations with powers and roots.**
3. **Do all multiplication and division operations from left to right.**
4. **Do all addition and subtraction operations from left to right.**

Evaluate (3 + 4) · 7

(3 + 4) · 7
7   · 7 = 49

Evaluate 12 ÷ (10 − 4)

12 ÷ (10 − 4)
12 ÷   6   = 2

Evaluate using the correct order of operations.

1. 5 · 5 + 9   (6 − 2) ÷ 4   2 · 7 + 6   14 − 4 ÷ 2
   25 + 9 = 34

2. 18 + 2 · 3   (21 − 7) · 7   (4 + 3) · 9   30 ÷ 3 · 2

3. 16 − 9 + 4   42 − 12 ÷ 6   3 · 5 − 10   12 · (2 − 1)

4. 50 ÷ (8 + 2)   5 + 6 · 3   12 ÷ 4 + 8   2 + 3 · 3

5. 10 − 3 ÷ 3   (15 − 10) ÷ 5   5 · 3 + 2   20 − 7 · 2

6. 16 ÷ 4 − 4   10 · 10 − 100   9 ÷ (2 + 1)   9 + 10 ÷ 5

7. (10 − 1) · 9   13 − 7 + 4   18 + 4 · 2   2 · 4 ÷ 2

8. (2 + 7) · 8   1 + (9 − 3)   8 · 6 + 9   12 ÷ 4 − 1

Evaluating Numerical Expressions

Some expressions contain powers and roots as well as parentheses and math operations. Refer to the rules on page 5 for the correct order of operations.

Evaluate $3^2 \div (7 - 4) + 2$

$$3^2 \div (7 - 4) + 2$$
$$3^2 \div 3 + 2$$
$$9 \div 3 + 2$$
$$3 + 2 = 5$$

Evaluate $(4 + 5) \div (2^2 - 1)$

$$(4 + 5) \div (2^2 - 1)$$
$$9 \div (4 - 1)$$
$$9 \div 3 = 3$$

Evaluate.

1. $5^2 \cdot (2 + 3) - 2^2$
   $25 \cdot 5 - 4$
   $125 - 4 = 121$

   $(9 - 6) \cdot (8 + 2)$

   $35 \div (7 - 2) \div \sqrt{49}$

2. $3 + 4 \cdot 4 - 15 \div 5$

   $8^2 + 6 \cdot (8 - 3)$

   $(9 + 9) \div (10 - 4)$

3. $10^2 - 20 \div (4 + 6)$

   $(11 - 3) \cdot \sqrt{16} + 9$

   $6^2 - (3 + 7) + 2^3$

4. $(12 + 8) \div (5 - 3)$

   $1 + 7^2 \cdot 4 + \sqrt{9}$

   $3^3 - 5 \cdot (7 - 5)$

5. $12^2 \div 3 \cdot 4 - \sqrt{144}$

   $(12 - 6) \cdot (8 + 2)$

   $(20 + 7) \div 3^2$

6. $9^2 + 7 \cdot (4 + 3)$

   $\sqrt{81} + 6^2 \div (7 - 1)$

   $15 \div 3 + 2 - 6$

7. $(30 + 5) \div (9 - 2)$

   $4^3 \div 2 - 2^2 \cdot 5$

   $6^3 \div (10 + 2) + 2$

8. $(29 - 5) \div \sqrt{36} + 3^2$

   $(2 + 3) \cdot (9 - 5)$

   $9^2 - (15 - 4) - 32$

9. $17 + 3 \div 3 \cdot \sqrt{25}$

   $42 \div 6 \cdot (18 - 9)$

   $(16 + 18) \div (19 - 2)$

10. $(33 - 6) \div 3^3$

    $4^2 + 2^3 \cdot 5$

    $(99 + 1) \div \sqrt{100}$

Writing Numerical Expressions

Sometimes you will need to write a numerical expression from the information given in a word problem in order to solve the problem. Replace the words with numbers and math operations before you evaluate the expression. Use the rules on page 5 for the correct order of operations.

Word Expression	Numerical Expression
four plus two minus five	4 + 2 − 5
six times seven divided by two	6 · 7 ÷ 2

If you want to add or subtract first, put the operation in parentheses.

Add five plus ten.	(5 + 10) ÷ 3
Then divide the result by three.	15 ÷ 3 = 5

Write a numerical expression for each word expression. Then evaluate.

1. three times seventeen
   3 · 17 = 51

   five plus seven minus four

2. eight divided by two times two

   thirteen minus seven

3. five squared plus nine

   one hundred plus sixty plus four

4. eighty-five divided by five

   twenty-seven plus three minus fifteen

5. forty-two divided by seven

   thirty times three divided by ten

6. Add thirteen plus seventeen. Then divide the result by ten.

7. Subtract nine from fifteen. Then multiply the result by six.

Write an expression for each problem. Then evaluate.

8. Angie and her 3 friends agreed to split the bill for lunch equally. The bill included salads for $14.00, drinks for $3.80, and a tip for $2.20. How much did each of the 4 people pay for lunch?

   Answer _____

9. The public library is open 3 mornings a week from 9 A.M. until noon. It is also open 4 afternoons a week from 1 P.M. to 6 P.M. and Saturdays from 9 A.M. until noon. How many hours a week is the public library open?

   Answer _____

7

Writing Algebraic Expressions

A numerical expression that contains a variable is called an algebraic expression. A variable is a letter that stands for an unknown number.

Word Expression	Algebraic Expression
three times a number	$3 \times n$ or $3 \cdot n$ or $3n$
five plus some number minus six	$5 + x - 6$
a number divided by seven	$y \div 7$ or $\dfrac{y}{7}$

Parentheses are used when addition or subtraction must be done first.

Find six plus a number. Then multiply the result by nine.	$(6 + z) \cdot 9$

Match each word expression with its equivalent algebraic expression.

__c__ 1. Four times the quantity x minus 9   a. $2z^2 + 5$

_____ 2. Sixteen divided by the number y b. $n(2 + 3)$

_____ 3. Two times z-squared plus five   c. $4x - 9$

_____ 4. n times the sum of two plus three   d. $\dfrac{16}{y}$

Write an algebraic expression for each problem. Use x for the variable.

5. a number times six   a number plus three
   6x

6. eight times a number   fifteen divided by some number

7. eleven plus a number   a number minus twelve

8. five times seven times some number   twenty-four minus a number plus six

9. thirty-two divided by a number   some number divided by seven

10. fifty times a number divided by three   four plus a number minus two

11. Find eight plus a number. Then divide the result by three.

12. Find thirty minus a number. Then multiply the result by seven.

Evaluating Algebraic Expressions

To evaluate an algebraic expression, substitute the given value of the variable in place of the variable. Evaluate the resulting numerical expression using the correct order of operations. Refer to the rules on page 5.

Evaluate $3 \cdot (4 - x)$ if $x = 1$.

$3 \cdot (4 - x)$
$3 \cdot (4 - 1)$
$3 \cdot 3 = 9$

Evaluate $x^2 - 3$ if $x = 4$.

$x^2 - 3$
$4^2 - 3$
$16 - 3 = 13$

Evaluate each expression if $n = 6$.

1. $n + 7$ \qquad\qquad $3n + 4$ \qquad\qquad $\dfrac{n}{2} - 1$ \qquad\qquad $15 - n$
   $6 + 7 = 13$

2. $n^2 - 5$ \qquad\qquad $(n - 2) \cdot 9$ \qquad\qquad $4n \div (3 + 1)$ \qquad\qquad $(18 - n) \cdot 2$

Evaluate each expression if $x = 7$.

3. $6x - 2$ \qquad\qquad $\dfrac{x}{7} \cdot 14$ \qquad\qquad $(x - 2) \cdot 8$ \qquad\qquad $(x - 5) \div 2$

4. $\dfrac{42}{x} + 9$ \qquad\qquad $(37 - x) \div 3$ \qquad\qquad $50 - 4x$ \qquad\qquad $x^3 - 25$

Evaluate each expression if $y = 1$.

5. $(y + 7) \div 2$ \qquad\qquad $\dfrac{4}{y} \cdot 9$ \qquad\qquad $18 - y$ \qquad\qquad $y^2 + 3$

6. $3y + 5$ \qquad\qquad $\dfrac{y}{6} \cdot 6$ \qquad\qquad $9 + y - 3$ \qquad\qquad $10 \cdot (5 - y)$

Evaluate each expression if $z = 12$.

7. $z - 6 \div 3$ \qquad\qquad $\dfrac{z}{4} - 2$ \qquad\qquad $(20 - z) \cdot 6$ \qquad\qquad $z^2 - 44$

8. $2 \cdot (z + 3)$ \qquad\qquad $(z + 6) \div 6$ \qquad\qquad $\dfrac{24}{z} \cdot 3$ \qquad\qquad $4z - 9$

Evaluating Algebraic Expressions

Some algebraic expressions contain two variables. Substitute the value of each variable for the variable. Then evaluate.

Evaluate $(x + y) \div 3$ if $x = 2$, $y = 7$.

$(x + y) \div 3$
$(2 + 7) \div 3$
$\quad 9 \div 3 = 3$

Evaluate $x^2 - y^2$ if $x = 5$, $y = 3$.

$x^2 - y^2$
$5^2 - 3^2$
$25 - 9 = 16$

Evaluate each expression if $x = 3$ and $y = 7$.

1. $2x + y$ $\qquad$ $9y - 32 + x$ $\qquad$ $x^2 - y$ $\qquad$ $(y - x) \cdot 4$
   $2(3) + 7$
   $\quad 6 + 7 = 13$

2. $\dfrac{y}{x} \cdot 3$ $\qquad$ $y^2 + 5 - x$ $\qquad$ $y \cdot (3x - 6)$ $\qquad$ $(4x + 2) \div y$

Evaluate each expression if $a = 8$ and $b = 4$.

3. $3a - b$ $\qquad$ $a^2 + b^2$ $\qquad$ $\dfrac{a}{b} \cdot 6$ $\qquad$ $(a + b) \cdot 7$

4. $\dfrac{2a}{4} \cdot b$ $\qquad$ $(4 + b) \div a$ $\qquad$ $5b - a$ $\qquad$ $b^3 \div a$

Evaluate each expression if $p = 5$ and $q = 10$.

5. $5p + q$ $\qquad$ $\dfrac{3q}{p}$ $\qquad$ $(p + q) \cdot 3$ $\qquad$ $p^2 \cdot q$

6. $8p \cdot (q - 8)$ $\qquad$ $6p + q$ $\qquad$ $q^2 - p^2$ $\qquad$ $\dfrac{p}{q} \cdot 10$

Evaluate each expression if $s = 6$ and $t = 2$.

7. $9t - s$ $\qquad$ $7 \cdot (s + t)$ $\qquad$ $s^2 + t^3$ $\qquad$ $s - 2t$

8. $\dfrac{s}{t} \cdot 3$ $\qquad$ $s^3 - 5t$ $\qquad$ $(8 - 2t) \cdot 4$ $\qquad$ $\dfrac{3t}{s} \cdot 15$

Solving Equations Using Basic Math Facts

An equation is a number sentence with an unknown number or variable. To solve an equation means to find the value of the variable that makes the equation true. Simple equations can be solved using basic math facts.

$x + 5 = 7$

| □ + 5 = 7 |
| 2 + 5 = 7 |
| x = 2 |

$y - 3 = 9$

| □ − 3 = 9 |
| 12 − 3 = 9 |
| y = 12 |

$5t = 30$

| 5 × □ = 30 |
| 5 × 6 = 30 |
| t = 6 |

$\frac{10}{n} = 2$

| 10 ÷ □ = 2 |
| 10 ÷ 5 = 2 |
| n = 5 |

Solve.

1. $x + 2 = 6$
   $4 + 2 = 6$
   $x = 4$

   $y - 7 = 1$

   $3p = 9$

   $\frac{5}{n} = 5$

2. $a - 2 = 10$

   $6q = 18$

   $\frac{4}{z} = 2$

   $r + 9 = 9$

3. $7x = 21$

   $\frac{b}{2} = 6$

   $y - 1 = 0$

   $6 + t = 11$

4. $\frac{p}{4} = 2$

   $9a = 72$

   $8 - n = 4$

   $2 + x = 6$

5. $9 + q = 15$

   $\frac{x}{3} = 3$

   $15 - y = 7$

   $4r = 16$

6. $12 - n = 9$

   $5 + p = 14$

   $5b = 20$

   $\frac{m}{5} = 4$

7. $8t = 48$

   $18 - x = 9$

   $r + 7 = 14$

   $\frac{n}{6} = 7$

8. $\frac{81}{p} = 9$

   $2q = 18$

   $5 + x = 13$

   $y - 8 = 6$

9. $8 + m = 15$

   $\frac{63}{n} = 7$

   $x - 6 = 11$

   $7y = 49$

Solving Equations with Two Variables

Some equations have two variables. If you know the value of one of the variables, use it in place of that variable. Then solve the equation for the unknown variable.

Solve $x + y = 6$ if $x = 3$.

$$x + y = 6$$
$$3 + y = 6$$
$$3 + 3 = 6$$
$$y = 3$$

Solve $y - x = 2$ if $x = 9$.

$$y - x = 2$$
$$y - 9 = 2$$
$$11 - 9 = 2$$
$$y = 11$$

Solve each equation if $x = 5$.

1. $x + y = 6$ $\quad\quad$ $1 = y - x$ $\quad\quad$ $\dfrac{x}{5} = y$ $\quad\quad$ $5x = y$
   $5 + y = 6$
   $y = 1$

2. $\dfrac{y}{x} = 7$ $\quad\quad$ $xy = 20$ $\quad\quad$ $x = 2 + y$ $\quad\quad$ $9 - y = x$

Solve each equation if $y = 10$.

3. $x - y = 4$ $\quad\quad$ $\dfrac{y}{2} = x$ $\quad\quad$ $5y = x$ $\quad\quad$ $y - 3 = x$

4. $3y = x$ $\quad\quad$ $y + 3 = x$ $\quad\quad$ $\dfrac{x}{9} = y$ $\quad\quad$ $y - x = 0$

Solve each equation if $a = 9$.

5. $ab = 18$ $\quad\quad$ $\dfrac{9}{a} = b$ $\quad\quad$ $1 = a - b$ $\quad\quad$ $a + 3 = b$

6. $b + 7 = a$ $\quad\quad$ $a = b - 7$ $\quad\quad$ $9a = b$ $\quad\quad$ $b = \dfrac{a}{3}$

Solve each equation if $b = 8$.

7. $a \div b = 3$ $\quad\quad$ $\dfrac{b}{2} = a$ $\quad\quad$ $b = a + 3$ $\quad\quad$ $9 - b = a$

8. $a = b - 2$ $\quad\quad$ $9b = a$ $\quad\quad$ $\dfrac{8}{b} = a$ $\quad\quad$ $a + b = 16$

Checking Up

Compare each set of numbers. Write < or >.

1. $-12 \square -11$ $0 \square -9$ $7 \square -7$ $2 \square 12$ $-4 \square -10$

Write each set of numbers in order from smallest to largest.

2. $-5, -7, 0$ $6, 0, -8$ $-4, -6, -1$ $3, 1, -1$

Write an expression for each word expression. Use b for the variable.

3. seven minus three   twenty-five plus six minus twelve

4. four times some number   eighty divided by a number

Evaluate each expression.

5. $5^2 \div (3 + 2) - 1$ $(6 + 3) - (5 - 1)$ $30 + 6 \div 2 - 5$

Evaluate each expression if $x = 9$ and $y = 3$.

6. $x^2 - 12$ $\dfrac{x}{3y}$ $5y - 10$ $(x - y) \div 2$

Solve.

7. $3x = 12$ $y + 9 = 14$ $\dfrac{15}{b} = 3$ $9 - n = 7$

Solve if $x = 4$.

8. $x = y + 1$ $y = x - 2$ $3x = y$ $9 - y = x$

Solve.

9. Josh is a driver for a messenger service. In one day he made 2 round trips of 16 miles each and 3 round trips of 18 miles each. He also went to the airport 3 times, traveling 11 miles each trip. How many miles did Josh drive that day?

    Answer _____

10. Thelma works for a florist. She received a shipment of 10 dozen roses. She had to throw away 20 flowers that were damaged in shipment. She divided the flowers she had left into 10 bunches with the same amount in each bunch. How many flowers were in each bunch?

    Answer _____

Adding Signed Numbers

When adding positive and negative numbers, or signed numbers, follow these rules.

Rule 1: To add two numbers with the same sign, add the numbers. Give the answer that sign.

Rule 2: To add numbers with different signs, find the difference between the numbers. Give the answer the sign of the larger number.

Rule 3: To add three or more signed numbers, add the positive numbers. Add the negative numbers. Then add the two totals. Use Rule 2 to find the sign.

Add $-6 + (-3)$

Use Rule 1.
$-6 + (-3) = -9$

Add $-13 + 7$

Use Rule 2.
$-13 + 7 = -6$

Add $36 + (-25) + (-5) + 4$

Use Rule 3.
$(-25) + (-5) = -30$
$36 + 4 = 40$
$40 + (-30) = 10$

Add.

1. $-10 + (-7)$ $-15 + 6$ $6 + (+9)$ $-12 + (-12) + (-5)$
   $-10 + (-7) = -17$

2. $-14 + 0$ $-18 + (-9)$ $-8 + (+3)$ $1 + (-9) + (-8)$

3. $10 + (-10)$ $13 + (-8)$ $-2 + (-5)$ $7 + (-16) + 4 + 2$

4. $-15 + 7$ $24 + (-12)$ $8 + (+8)$ $-19 + (-2) + (-3)$

5. $20 + (-8)$ $-9 + (-9)$ $13 + (-13)$ $-4 + 4 + (-8)$

6. $0 + (-22)$ $-5 + (-5)$ $-30 + (-9)$ $25 + (-5) + (-10)$

7. $-11 + 6$ $7 + (-7)$ $-6 + 15$ $1 + (-6) + 5 + (-9)$

8. $-2 + (-5)$ $4 + (-14)$ $-13 + (-15)$ $21 + (-13) + (-12)$

9. $32 + (-16)$ $7 + (-21)$ $-35 + (+19)$ $-3 + (-19) + (-6) + 9$

10. $-12 + (-26)$ $-18 + (+15)$ $-13 + 13$ $4 + (-6) + 4 + (-12)$

Subtracting Signed Numbers

When subtracting signed numbers, follow this rule.

To subtract signed numbers, change the sign of the number being subtracted. Then add.

Subtract −3 − (+11)

$$-3 - (+11)$$
$$(-3) + (-11) = -14$$

Subtract −10 − (−10)

$$-10 - (-10)$$
$$-10 + (+10) = 0$$

Subtract 0 − (−2)

$$0 - (-2)$$
$$0 + (+2) = 2$$

Subtract.

1. −10 − (+6)   −7 − (−6)   15 − (−2)   −8 − 0
   −10 + (−6) = −16

2. 7 − (+14)   −16 − (+4)   19 − (−7)   −3 − (−15)

3. 0 − (−3)   −5 − (−5)   −2 − (−16)   13 − (+11)

4. −8 − (+10)   11 − (+11)   12 − (−12)   −15 − 0

5. 18 − (+7)   22 − (−5)   4 − (−17)   −2 − (−6)

6. −10 − (−15)   3 − (+7)   0 − 24   −18 − (−25)

7. 16 − (+4)   −30 − (+15)   −17 − (−2)   40 − 0

8. 22 − (−3)   −25 − (−8)   −6 − (−29)   −15 − (−15)

9. 1 − (−2)   −10 − (−20)   2 − (+6)   7 − (+19)

10. 33 − (+11)   −35 − (−15)   −26 − (+13)   9 − (+24)

11. −42 − (−15)   3 − (+24)   16 − (+40)   27 − (+27)

12. 0 − (−17)   −18 − (−1)   −2 − (+17)   30 − (+39)

13. −50 − (−25)   13 − (+17)   14 − (−14)   −23 − (−23)

Adding and Subtracting Signed Numbers

When adding and subtracting three or more signed numbers, change the sign of any numbers being subtracted. Then follow addition Rule 3 on page 14.

Add and subtract −9 + 6 − (−3)

Change the sign of the number being subtracted.	Add the positive numbers.	Add the positive and the negative numbers.
−9 + 6 − (−3) −9 + 6 + 3	6 + 3 = 9	−9 + 9 = 0

Add and subtract.

1. −5 + 7 − (−1)   7 − (+5) + 2   −10 + (−7) + (−6) − 2
   −5 + 7 + 1
   −5 + 8 = 3

2. 17 − 32 + (−16)   −9 + 15 − (−6)   1 − (−2) + (−3)

3. −14 − (−16) + 2   15 − (−9) + (−2)   −6 + 2 − (−14) + (−6)

4. 2 + 5 − (−9)   −13 + (−12) + 1   −11 + (−2) − (+13)

5. −16 − (−8) + 2   16 + (−16) − 12   14 + (−16) − (+14) − 9

6. −6 − (+4) − 10   −18 − (−12) + 4   −13 − 12 + (−8)

7. 5 + (+5) + (+10)   −13 − (−11) − 15   −20 + (−16) + (−5) + (−3)

8. −4 − (+2) + (−6)   7 − (+2) − (−9)   8 − (+2) − (+4) − (+2)

9. −12 − (+6) − (−9)   −15 − (+8) − (−6)   −6 + 3 − (−10)

10. 5 − (−5) − (+5)   32 − (+14) − (+20)   1 − (−1) + (2)

Solving Addition Equations

To solve an addition equation, subtract the same number from each side of the equation to leave the variable by itself on one side of the equal sign and the value of the variable on the other side. Check by substituting the value of the variable in the equation.

Solve $x + 12 = 16$

Subtract 12 from each side and solve.	Check by substituting 4 for x.
$x + 12 = 16$ $x + 12 - 12 = 16 - 12$ $x = 4$	$x + 12 = 16$ $4 + 12 = 16$ $16 = 16$

Solve. Check.

1. $x + 5 = 12$ $\qquad$ $x + 13 = -1$ $\qquad$ $14 + x = -2$ $\qquad$ $9 + x = 12$
   $x + 5 - 5 = 12 - 5$
   $x = 7$

2. $15 + x = 3$ $\qquad$ $x + 9 = 14$ $\qquad$ $x + 10 = 6$ $\qquad$ $13 + x = 33$

3. $14 + x = -9$ $\qquad$ $x + 2 = -1$ $\qquad$ $20 + x = 35$ $\qquad$ $x + 5 = 0$

4. $x + 6 = 13$ $\qquad$ $x + 5 = -5$ $\qquad$ $x + 4 = 1$ $\qquad$ $9 + x = -5$

5. $3 + x = -5$ $\qquad$ $18 + x = 32$ $\qquad$ $22 + x = -8$ $\qquad$ $x + 32 = -12$

6. $x + 16 = -9$ $\qquad$ $x + 17 = -17$ $\qquad$ $19 + x = -4$ $\qquad$ $30 + x = 69$

7. $x + 12 = 6$ $\qquad$ $x + 11 = -10$ $\qquad$ $8 + x = 9$ $\qquad$ $14 + x = -14$

8. $21 + x = 7$ $\qquad$ $17 + x = 34$ $\qquad$ $x + 15 = 2$ $\qquad$ $x + 20 = -40$

9. $x + 27 = -17$ $\qquad$ $x + 1 = 15$ $\qquad$ $24 + x = 12$ $\qquad$ $x + 18 = 30$

Solving Subtraction Equations

To solve a subtraction equation, add the same number to both sides of the equation. Check by substituting the value of the variable in the equation.

Solve $x - 10 = -9$

Add 10 to each side and solve.	Check by substituting 1 for x.
$x - 10 = -9$ $x - 10 + 10 = -9 + 10$ $x = 1$	$x - 10 = -9$ $1 - 10 = -9$ $-9 = -9$

Solve. Check.

1. $x - 2 = 3$ $x - 5 = -6$ $x - 6 = 12$ $x - 1 = 1$
$x - 2 + 2 = 3 + 2$
$x = 5$

2. $x - 7 = -1$ $x - 9 = -3$ $x - 10 = -17$ $x - 15 = -4$

3. $x - 11 = -2$ $x - 4 = -9$ $x - 12 = -3$ $x - 17 = 2$

4. $x - 3 = 4$ $x - 8 = 6$ $x - 6 = -11$ $x - 18 = -12$

5. $x - 2 = -5$ $x - 3 = -9$ $x - 19 = 20$ $x - 6 = -5$

6. $x - 7 = 10$ $x - 25 = -7$ $x - 8 = 3$ $x - 1 = -3$

7. $x - 36 = -40$ $x - 12 = 40$ $x - 4 = -37$ $x - 18 = 42$

8. $x - 50 = 32$ $x - 17 = -35$ $x - 45 = 15$ $x - 14 = -20$

9. $x - 11 = -5$ $x - 1 = 37$ $x - 13 = 54$ $x - 30 = -50$

Checking Up

Add or subtract.

1. $-9 + (-6)$ $6 - (+6)$ $18 + (-9) + 7$ $15 - (-5) + 6 + (-1)$

2. $-12 + 0$ $10 + (-7)$ $-13 - (-13) + 2$ $-15 + (-5) + (-3)$

3. $12 + (-4)$ $-6 + (-14)$ $-17 - (-4) + 5$ $0 - (-10) + 1 - 6$

4. $-8 - (+7)$ $3 + (-21)$ $-1 + (-11) + 4$ $32 - (+15) + 2$

5. $-11 - (+18)$ $13 + (-16)$ $-9 - (-9) + 8$ $-2 + (-8) + 7 - (-2)$

6. $-25 + (-7)$ $-36 - (+12)$ $2 - (-15) + 1$ $4 + (-11) + (-20)$

Solve. Check.

7. $x + 2 = 7$ $x + 5 = -2$ $x - 6 = 3$ $x - 9 = 9$

8. $3 + x = -4$ $x - 15 = -20$ $7 + x = -9$ $x - 1 = -1$

9. $x - 4 = -8$ $x + 10 = -15$ $6 + x = 14$ $12 + x = 6$

10. $x - 11 = 10$ $x - 8 = -2$ $x - 16 = -14$ $x + 13 = 25$

11. $x + 1 = -7$ $11 + x = 17$ $4 + x = 2$ $x - 3 = 4$

12. $x + 9 = -9$ $x + 13 = 5$ $x - 10 = 2$ $x - 7 = 30$

Multiplying Signed Numbers

When multiplying signed numbers, follow these rules. Notice that multiplication is shown using parentheses around one or both signed numbers to avoid confusing operation signs and negative number signs.

Rule 1: To multiply numbers with the same sign, multiply and give the answer a positive sign.

Rule 2: To multiply numbers with different signs, multiply and give the answer a negative sign.

Rule 3: To multiply several signed numbers, multiply the numbers two at a time using Rules 1 and 2.

Multiply (−3) (−6)

Use Rule 1.
(−3) (−6) = 18

Multiply (4) (−2)

Use Rule 2.
(4) (−2) = −8

Multiply (−5) (5) (−2)

Use Rule 3.
(−5) (5) = −25
(−25) (−2) = 50

Multiply.

1. −9 (3)   (−5) (−6)   4 (−8)   (8) (−9)
   (−9) (3) = −27

2. −1 (−5)   −7 (2)   9 (−12)   (11) (−2)

3. 2 (1)   −3 (−4)   6 (−7)   −10 (−11)

4. 12 (9)   15 (−10)   −20 (−6)   16 (−3)

5. −6 (8)   −9 (9)   −7 (−11)   11 (−2)

6. (9) (−2) (3)   (−13) (−7) (2)   (3) (5) (−3)

7. (−1) (20) (−4)   (−2) (−3) (7)   (10) (−10) (−6)

8. (4) (13) (0)   (−9) (−9) (−2)   (14) (−1) (3)

9. (−4) (4) (3) (−4) (12) (2) (−2) (7)   (−8) (−9) (−1) (−3)

Dividing Signed Numbers

When dividing signed numbers, follow these rules.

Rule 1: To divide numbers with the same sign, divide and give the answer a positive sign.

Rule 2: To divide numbers with different signs, divide and give the answer a negative sign.

Divide $\dfrac{-15}{-3}$

> Use Rule 1.
> $\dfrac{-15}{-3} = 5$

Divide $\dfrac{18}{-6}$

> Use Rule 2.
> $\dfrac{18}{-6} = -3$

Divide $\dfrac{-20}{4}$

> Use Rule 2.
> $\dfrac{-20}{4} = -5$

Divide.

1. $\dfrac{-12}{3} = -4$ $\dfrac{-14}{-2}$ $\dfrac{20}{-10}$ $\dfrac{-25}{5}$

2. $\dfrac{42}{6}$ $\dfrac{-36}{6}$ $\dfrac{32}{-4}$ $\dfrac{90}{9}$

3. $\dfrac{48}{8}$ $\dfrac{52}{-13}$ $\dfrac{-63}{7}$ $\dfrac{72}{9}$

4. $\dfrac{60}{15}$ $\dfrac{-16}{4}$ $\dfrac{-10}{10}$ $\dfrac{30}{3}$

5. $\dfrac{-34}{17}$ $\dfrac{81}{-9}$ $\dfrac{24}{-6}$ $\dfrac{27}{9}$

6. $\dfrac{35}{7}$ $\dfrac{40}{-5}$ $\dfrac{-36}{9}$ $\dfrac{-49}{7}$

7. $\dfrac{9}{3}$ $\dfrac{-18}{2}$ $\dfrac{15}{-5}$ $\dfrac{-8}{4}$

8. $\dfrac{11}{1}$ $\dfrac{-12}{-12}$ $\dfrac{-20}{10}$ $\dfrac{-21}{7}$

9. $\dfrac{24}{8}$ $\dfrac{-2}{1}$ $\dfrac{-28}{-14}$ $\dfrac{13}{13}$

10. $\dfrac{44}{-11}$ $\dfrac{-30}{3}$ $\dfrac{32}{4}$ $\dfrac{22}{-2}$

11. $\dfrac{50}{25}$ $\dfrac{75}{-3}$ $\dfrac{-63}{9}$ $\dfrac{19}{1}$

Adding, Subtracting, Multiplying, and Dividing Signed Numbers

Use the rules for adding, subtracting, multiplying, and dividing signed numbers.

1. $3 + (-4)$ $7 - (-2)$ $8(-5)$ $\dfrac{30}{-2}$
   $3 + (-4) = -1$

2. $-9 - (-9)$ $-10 + (-8)$ $\dfrac{-24}{6}$ $(-12)(3)(-2)$

3. $\dfrac{45}{-9}$ $13(-4)$ $-5 + (-10)$ $7 - (+9)$

4. $(-8)(-3)(-4)$ $\dfrac{-36}{-6}$ $19 - (-12)$ $-21 + (10)$

5. $15 + (-12)$ $1 - (+1)$ $9(-6)$ $\dfrac{25}{-5}$

6. $-15(-4)$ $\dfrac{-100}{25}$ $-26 - (-13)$ $16 + (-29)$

7. $6 - (+17)$ $(-3)(-30)(3)$ $42 + (-19)$ $\dfrac{-81}{9}$

8. $\dfrac{20}{-4}$ $-22 - (+33)$ $-4(32)$ $-8 + (-8)$

Use the rules for signed numbers and the correct order of operations.

9. $\dfrac{30}{6} - 2(9)$ $-5(4) + 3 - 7$ $18 - 6(4)$ $32 + (-9)(-9)$
   $5 - 18 = -13$

10. $49 - 7(+7)$ $\dfrac{-14}{7} + 3(-2)$ $13 + 5(-2)$ $6(-3) - 2(-7)$

11. $\dfrac{54}{9} + 8(-10)$ $-18(-4) - 62$ $35 + \dfrac{14}{2} - 5$ $40(-3) + 100$

12. $\dfrac{-80}{8} - \dfrac{15}{3}$ $16(-2) + 32$ $84 - 18(4)$ $-8(9) - 5(7)$

13. $18 - \dfrac{45}{5}$ $\dfrac{42}{-7} + 6(-8)$ $100 - 5(-20)$ $-\dfrac{50}{25} - 2(-1)$

Solving Multiplication Equations

To solve a multiplication equation, divide each side of the equation by the same number. Follow the rules on page 21 for dividing signed numbers. Check by substituting the value of the variable in the equation.

Solve $3x = -42$

Divide each side by 3.	Check by substituting –14 for x.
$3x = -42$	$3x = -42$
$\dfrac{3x}{3} = \dfrac{-42}{3}$	$3(-14) = -42$
$x = -14$	$-42 = -42$

Solve. Check.

1. $-5x = 20$ $\quad\quad$ $-4x = -16$ $\quad\quad$ $6x = 24$ $\quad\quad$ $9x = -18$
   $\dfrac{-5x}{-5} = \dfrac{20}{-5}$
   $x = -4$

2. $12x = 24$ $\quad\quad$ $-10x = 30$ $\quad\quad$ $8x = -48$ $\quad\quad$ $-7x = 49$

3. $5x = 25$ $\quad\quad$ $-3x = -18$ $\quad\quad$ $-2x = 16$ $\quad\quad$ $11x = 33$

4. $-15x = 45$ $\quad\quad$ $-4x = 24$ $\quad\quad$ $5x = -15$ $\quad\quad$ $14x = -28$

5. $7x = 42$ $\quad\quad$ $10x = -50$ $\quad\quad$ $-12x = -36$ $\quad\quad$ $-6x = 54$

6. $-9x = -63$ $\quad\quad$ $-5x = 5$ $\quad\quad$ $11x = 0$ $\quad\quad$ $2x = -12$

7. $-4x = 8$ $\quad\quad$ $7x = -21$ $\quad\quad$ $8x = 24$ $\quad\quad$ $-13x = -52$

8. $3x = -9$ $\quad\quad$ $-10x = 100$ $\quad\quad$ $-14x = -28$ $\quad\quad$ $6x = 48$

9. $-12x = 12$ $\quad\quad$ $-9x = -81$ $\quad\quad$ $5x = -40$ $\quad\quad$ $-2x = 10$

Solving Division Equations

To solve division equations, multiply each side of the equation by the same number. Follow the rules on page 20 for multiplying signed numbers. Check by substituting the value of the variable in the equation.

Solve $\frac{x}{-9} = 2$

Multiply each side by −9.

$$\frac{x}{-9} = 2$$

$$-9\left(\frac{x}{-9}\right) = -9(2)$$

$$x = -18$$

Check by substituting −18 for x.

$$\frac{x}{-9} = 2$$

$$\frac{-18}{-9} = 2$$

$$2 = 2$$

Solve. Check.

1. $\frac{x}{5} = -6$ $\qquad$ $\frac{x}{-4} = -8$ $\qquad$ $\frac{x}{3} = 12$ $\qquad$ $\frac{x}{-6} = -3$

   $5\left(\frac{x}{5}\right) = 5(-6)$

   $x = -30$

2. $\frac{x}{10} = 8$ $\qquad$ $\frac{x}{-7} = -4$ $\qquad$ $\frac{x}{-5} = 15$ $\qquad$ $\frac{x}{8} = -7$

3. $\frac{x}{-4} = 9$ $\qquad$ $\frac{x}{9} = -2$ $\qquad$ $\frac{x}{-10} = -12$ $\qquad$ $\frac{x}{6} = 10$

4. $\frac{x}{3} = 1$ $\qquad$ $\frac{x}{2} = -5$ $\qquad$ $\frac{x}{4} = -6$ $\qquad$ $\frac{x}{-5} = -3$

5. $\frac{x}{-10} = 14$ $\qquad$ $\frac{x}{7} = -8$ $\qquad$ $\frac{x}{8} = 10$ $\qquad$ $\frac{x}{-9} = -5$

6. $\frac{x}{-2} = -7$ $\qquad$ $\frac{x}{3} = -3$ $\qquad$ $\frac{x}{-9} = -8$ $\qquad$ $\frac{x}{12} = 2$

7. $\frac{x}{11} = 4$ $\qquad$ $\frac{x}{-10} = -1$ $\qquad$ $\frac{x}{-4} = -12$ $\qquad$ $\frac{x}{5} = -11$

8. $\frac{x}{-3} = -15$ $\qquad$ $\frac{x}{9} = 13$ $\qquad$ $\frac{x}{-6} = -9$ $\qquad$ $\frac{x}{8} = 6$

9. $\frac{x}{5} = -5$ $\qquad$ $\frac{x}{-7} = -7$ $\qquad$ $\frac{x}{10} = 8$ $\qquad$ $\frac{x}{12} = -3$

Checking Up

Add, subtract, multiply, or divide.

1. $-5 + (-3)$ $18 - (-9)$ $\dfrac{32}{-8} - 4$ $15(-4)$

2. $\dfrac{-20}{4}$ $-8(-6) + 2$ $13(-10)$ $-30 - (-12)$

3. $-42 - 14$ $\dfrac{45}{5} - 3$ $(12)(-12)(-2)$ $36 - (+30)$

4. $\dfrac{16}{-2}$ $(-2)(-7)(-3)$ $19 + (-3)(5)$ $-7 - (-7)$

5. $0 - (-13)$ $\dfrac{63}{7} + 3(2)$ $12(-1)$ $-\dfrac{24}{6} - 5$

6. $18 - 6(3) + 5$ $\dfrac{100}{-10}$ $-4(-5) - (-9)$ $-1 + (-7)$

7. $\dfrac{-81}{9}$ $8 - (+8)$ $-9 - (+12) + (-12)$ $-7(5)$

8. $8(-8) + 32$ $20 - (-10)$ $\dfrac{44}{-11}$ $0 + (-2) - (+2)$

Solve.

9. $x + 8 = 8$ $-6x = 54$ $x - 7 = 0$ $\dfrac{x}{9} = -3$

10. $10x = -30$ $\dfrac{x}{5} = -7$ $12 + x = 36$ $x - 14 = 20$

11. $x + 11 = 10$ $x - 19 = 32$ $\dfrac{x}{-4} = 17$ $12x = 48$

12. $\dfrac{x}{15} = -2$ $30x = -30$ $1 + x = -6$ $x - 16 = -64$

13. $x + 25 = 5$ $\dfrac{x}{7} = -9$ $x - 22 = 11$ $14x = 28$

14. $x - 27 = -10$ $24x = -96$ $\dfrac{x}{-6} = -5$ $18 + x = 50$

Solving Fraction Equations

To solve a fraction equation, multiply each side of the equation by the reciprocal of the fraction. The reciprocal is the fraction inverted, or turned upside down.

Solve $\frac{2}{9}x = 4$

Multiply each side by the reciprocal of $\frac{2}{9}$.	Cancel and then divide.	Check by substituting 18 for x.
$\frac{9}{2} \cdot \frac{2}{9}x = 4 \cdot \frac{9}{2}$	$\frac{\cancel{9}}{\cancel{2}} \cdot \frac{\cancel{2}}{\cancel{9}}x = 4 \cdot \frac{9}{2}$ $x = \frac{36}{2}$ $x = 18$	$\frac{2}{9} \cdot 18 = 4$ $\frac{36}{9} = 4$ $4 = 4$

Solve. Check.

1. $-\frac{3}{8}y = 9$

   $-\frac{8}{3}\left(-\frac{3}{8}y\right) = 9\left(-\frac{8}{3}\right)$

   $y = -\frac{72}{3}$

   $y = -24$

   $\frac{4}{9}x = -4$

   $-\frac{2}{5}x = 10$

2. $\frac{5}{12}y = -15$ $\quad\quad\quad\quad\quad\quad\quad$ $\frac{1}{4}x = 6$ $\quad\quad\quad\quad\quad\quad\quad$ $-\frac{6}{7}x = 36$

3. $\frac{1}{3}y = -3$ $\quad\quad\quad\quad\quad\quad\quad$ $-\frac{7}{10}y = -14$ $\quad\quad\quad\quad\quad\quad$ $\frac{5}{6}y = 20$

4. $\frac{7}{11}x = 21$ $\quad\quad\quad\quad\quad\quad\quad$ $-\frac{3}{13}x = 9$ $\quad\quad\quad\quad\quad\quad$ $\frac{9}{15}x = -18$

5. $\frac{11}{20}y = 33$ $\quad\quad\quad\quad\quad\quad\quad$ $-\frac{2}{3}y = 10$ $\quad\quad\quad\quad\quad\quad$ $\frac{1}{18}x = 5$

Solving Two-Step Equations

To solve some equations, you may need to use more than one operation. Be sure to add or subtract first. Then multiply or divide.

Solve $6x - 3 = -9$

Add 3 to both sides.	Divide both sides by 6.	Check by substituting −1 for x.
$6x - 3 + 3 = -9 + 3$ $6x = -6$	$\dfrac{6x}{6} = \dfrac{-6}{6}$ $x = -1$	$6(-1) - 3 = -9$ $-6 - 3 = -9$ $-9 = -9$

Solve. Check.

1. $\quad 4x + 2 = 10$ $\qquad\qquad\qquad\qquad \dfrac{x}{6} - 3 = 1 \qquad\qquad\qquad 8 - 2x = -16$
   $4x + 2 - 2 = 10 - 2$
   $\qquad\quad 4x = 8$
   $\qquad\quad \dfrac{4x}{4} = \dfrac{8}{4}$
   $\qquad\qquad x = 2$

2. $\dfrac{5}{7}x - 3 = 2 \qquad\qquad\qquad -6y + 2 = 8 \qquad\qquad\qquad \dfrac{y}{5} - 1 = 0$

3. $\dfrac{3}{4}y - 3 = 3 \qquad\qquad\qquad 9 - 3x = 36 \qquad\qquad\qquad \dfrac{y}{3} - 5 = 10$

4. $4 + 8x = -4 \qquad\qquad\qquad \dfrac{1}{2}y + 2 = -2 \qquad\qquad\qquad \dfrac{y}{7} - 8 = -9$

5. $18y - 6 = 12 \qquad\qquad\qquad -5 + 10x = 15 \qquad\qquad\qquad \dfrac{2}{3}y + 1 = 3$

Solving Two-Step Fraction Equations

The variable in a fraction equation may be in either the numerator or the denominator.

$$\frac{3x}{5} = 6 \qquad \frac{12}{x} = 4$$

To solve these equations, use two steps. Multiply each side of the equation by the denominator. Then divide.

Solve $\frac{5x}{9} = 5$

Multiply by 9. Then divide.	Check by substituting 9 for x.
$(9)\frac{5x}{9} = 5(9)$ $5x = 45$ $x = \frac{45}{5}$ $x = 9$	$\frac{5 \cdot 9}{9} = 5$ $\frac{45}{9} = 5$ $5 = 5$

Solve $\frac{2}{x} = 2$

Multiply by x. Then divide.	Check by substituting 1 for x.
$(x)\frac{2}{x} = 2(x)$ $2 = 2x$ $\frac{2}{2} = x$ $1 = x$	$\frac{2}{1} = 2$ $2 = 2$

Solve. Check.

1. $\frac{3x}{4} = -9$ $\qquad\qquad\qquad$ $\frac{9}{x} = 3$ $\qquad\qquad\qquad$ $-\frac{2x}{3} = 4$
    $(4)\frac{3x}{4} = -9(4)$
    $3x = -36$
    $x = -12$

2. $\frac{4x}{7} = 16$ $\qquad\qquad\qquad$ $\frac{10}{x} = -5$ $\qquad\qquad\qquad$ $\frac{26}{x} = 13$

3. $\frac{6x}{10} = -12$ $\qquad\qquad\qquad$ $-\frac{4}{x} = 1$ $\qquad\qquad\qquad$ $\frac{7x}{8} = 7$

4. $-\frac{5x}{6} = 10$ $\qquad\qquad\qquad$ $\frac{14}{x} = -2$ $\qquad\qquad\qquad$ $-\frac{18x}{3} = 12$

5. $\frac{8x}{12} = -4$ $\qquad\qquad\qquad$ $\frac{15}{x} = 3$ $\qquad\qquad\qquad$ $-\frac{54}{x} = 3$

Checking Up

Solve each equation. Check.

1. $\frac{1}{9}x = 3$ $-\frac{2}{3}y = 6$ $\frac{3}{7}x = -9$

2. $\frac{4}{5}x = -8$ $\frac{1}{10}y = 2$ $-\frac{3}{4}y = 6$

3. $-\frac{3}{4}y + 1 = -14$ $7x - 10 = -3$ $14 - 5x = -1$

4. $5x - 6 = 9$ $3 - 9y = -6$ $\frac{y}{8} - 2 = 3$

5. $\frac{3}{5}x + 4 = 10$ $5 - 2y = 1$ $\frac{x}{9} + 10 = 20$

6. $\frac{5x}{6} = -10$ $-\frac{2x}{3} = 4$ $\frac{7}{9}y = 21$

7. $\frac{12}{x} = 3$ $\frac{15}{y} = -5$ $\frac{8}{x} = 1$

8. $\frac{1y}{2} = -15$ $-\frac{22}{x} = 2$ $\frac{5y}{12} = 5$

29

Using Formulas to Solve Distance Problems

Formulas are another kind of algebraic equation. Substitute the information you have for the variables in the formula and solve for the unknown.

Problems involving distance (*d*), rate (*r*), and time (*t*) are solved using the distance formulas.

$d = rt$ to solve for distance

$r = \dfrac{d}{t}$ to solve for rate

$t = \dfrac{d}{r}$ to solve for time

An airplane is traveling at 500 miles per hour (mph). How far can it travel in 3 hours?

Use the formula for how far the airplane can travel (distance).	Substitute the numbers in the formula. Solve.
$d = rt$	$d = 500 \times 3$ $d = 1{,}500$ miles

Solve.

1. Sarah drove 300 miles averaging 50 miles per hour. How long did it take her to travel 300 miles at this rate?

   $t = \dfrac{d}{r}$

   $t = \dfrac{300}{50}$

   $t = 6$ hours

   Answer ____6 hours____

2. It is 100 miles from Center City to Plainville. How fast must you drive to get from one city to the other in 2 hours?

   Answer _____

3. If you walked at a rate of 4 mph, how long would it take you to walk 12 miles?

   Answer _____

4. The Thompsons drove an average of 60 mph for $6\tfrac{1}{2}$ hours on the first day of their vacation. How many miles did they drive on the first day?

   Answer _____

5. If an airplane travels nonstop 3,000 miles across the United States, how many miles an hour does the airplane average if it makes the trip in 5 hours?

   Answer _____

6. A boat is traveling at 15 mph in still water. How far will it travel in $\tfrac{1}{2}$ hour?

   Answer _____

Using Formulas to Solve Interest Problems

Problems involving simple interest (*i*), principal (*p*), rate (*r*), and time (*t*) are solved using the interest formulas.

$i = prt$ to solve for simple interest earned or owed

$p = \dfrac{i}{rt}$ to solve for the principal, the amount invested or borrowed

$r = \dfrac{i}{pt}$ to solve for the yearly (annual) interest rate

$t = \dfrac{i}{pr}$ to solve for the time in years

Jake borrowed $300 at a yearly interest rate of 6%. How much simple interest will he owe if he pays back the loan at the end of 6 months?

Use the formula for interest.	Substitute the numbers in the formula.	Change the percent and the time to decimals. Solve.
$i = prt$	$i = \$300 \times 6\% \times 6 \text{ months}$	$i = \$300 \times .06 \times .5$ $i = \$9.00$

Solve.

1. If you earn $20 simple interest in 1 year on a deposit of $500 in a savings account, what is the annual interest rate?

    $r = \dfrac{i}{pt}$

    $r = \dfrac{\$20}{\$500 \times 1 \text{ year}}$

    $r = 20 \div 500 = .04$

    $r = 4\%$

    Answer _____4%_____

2. Jane took out a $5,000 loan to buy a car. How much simple interest will she pay if she is charged 10% annually and repays the loan at the end of 2 years?

    Answer _____

3. How much money will you need to deposit to earn $75 in simple interest in 6 months if your bank pays 5% annually?

    Answer _____

4. After 1 year, Bob paid $14 simple interest on some money he borrowed at an annual rate of 7%. How much did Bob borrow?

    Answer _____

5. After 3 months, Al paid $15 simple interest on a $300 loan. What was the annual interest rate?

    Answer _____

6. How many years must you leave $1,000 in a savings account to earn $120 in simple interest if the bank pays 6% annually?

    Answer _____

Using Formulas to Solve Cost Problems

Problems involving total cost (c), number of units (n), and cost per unit (r) are solved using the cost formulas.

$c = nr$ to solve for the total cost

$n = \dfrac{c}{r}$ to solve for the number of units

$r = \dfrac{c}{n}$ to solve for the cost per unit (rate)

The total cost of a shipment of textbooks is $1,200. If each book costs $15, how many books are in the shipment?

Use the formula to find the number of units.	Substitute the numbers in the formula. Solve.
$n = \dfrac{c}{r}$	$n = \dfrac{1200}{15}$ $n = 80$

Solve.

1. If you buy 25 pounds of pecans for $5 per pound, what is the total cost?

   $c = nr$
   $c = 25 \times 5$
   $c = \$125$

   Answer _____$125_____

2. If a 50-pound bag of potatoes costs $12.50, how much does 1 pound of potatoes cost?

   Answer _____

3. The total cost of a case of film is $48. If each roll of film costs $2, how many rolls of film are in the case?

   Answer _____

4. Howard's Nursery sells rose bushes 4 for $18. How much does 1 rose bush cost?

   Answer _____

5. An office supply store sells packages of pencils for $.75 each. How much will 10 packages cost?

   Answer _____

6. The Harper Business Association bought tickets to the circus for local school children. If each ticket costs $4 and the association spent $200, how many tickets did they buy?

   Answer _____

Choosing a Formula

On some tests, there are multiple-choice problems where you must choose the correct way to set up a problem in order to find the answer.

Circle the letter next to the correct way to set up the formula. Then solve.

1. A car is traveling at an average rate of 45 mph. How far will it travel in 5 hours?
   a. $\frac{45}{5}$
   b. $\frac{5}{45}$
   ⓒ. 45×5

   Answer _____ $45 \times 5 = 225$ miles _____

2. How much money would you need to deposit to earn $35 in simple interest in 1 year if your bank pays 3.5% annually?
   a. $35 \times .035$
   b. $\frac{35}{.035}$
   c. $\frac{.035}{35}$

   Answer _____

3. A hardware store ordered 4 dozen boxes of heavy-duty staples for a total cost of $43.20. What was the cost of 1 dozen boxes?
   a. 4×43.20
   b. $\frac{43.20}{4}$
   c. $43.20 + 4$

   Answer _____

4. If you walked at a rate of 5 miles per hour, how far would you walk in 2 hours?
   a. $5(2)$
   b. $2 + 5(2)$
   c. $\frac{5}{2}$

   Answer _____

5. Mary borrowed $500 for 9 months. Her bank charges 9% simple interest annually. How much simple interest will she owe after 9 months?
   a. $500 \times 9 \times 9$
   b. $500 \times .09 \times .75$
   c. $500 + .09(500)$

   Answer _____

6. Felipe's son was selling calendars at $3.50 each for a school project. If his son sold 52 calendars, how much money did Felipe's son collect?
   a. $\frac{52}{3.50}$
   b. $\frac{3.50}{52}$
   c. 3.50×52

   Answer _____

7. A boat traveled 100 miles in 5 hours. What was the speed of the boat?
   a. $\frac{100}{5}$
   b. 5×100
   c. $\frac{5}{100}$

   Answer _____

8. If you deposit $100 in a savings account that pays 5% simple interest, how many years will it take to earn $100 in interest?
   a. $\frac{100}{.05} + 100$
   b. $\frac{100}{(100)(.05)}$
   c. $100 + (.05)(100)$

   Answer _____

Using the Perimeter Formula

The formula for finding the perimeter of a rectangle, $P = 2l + 2w$, can also be used to find the length of one side. To find the length of the unknown side, subtract the lengths of the known sides from the perimeter.

The perimeter of a rectangle is 16 feet. Find the width if the length is 5 feet.

	Substitute.	Subtract.	Divide.
w $l = 5$ ft.	$P = 2l + 2w$ $16 = 2(5) + 2w$ $16 = 10 + 2w$	$16 - 10 = 10 - 10 + 2w$ $6 = 2w$	$\dfrac{6}{2} = \dfrac{2w}{2}$ $3 = w$

Solve.

1. The perimeter of a rectangle is 24 feet. Find the length if the width is 2 feet.

   $P = 2l + 2w$
   $24 = 2l + 2(2)$
   $24 = 2l + 4$
   $24 - 4 = 2l + 4 - 4$
   $20 = 2l$
   $\dfrac{20}{2} = \dfrac{2l}{2}$
   $10 = l$

   Answer _____10 feet_____

2. The perimeter of a rectangle is 50 centimeters. Find the length if the width is 12 centimeters.

   Answer _____

3. The perimeter of a rectangular garden is 100 feet. Find the width if the length is 35 feet.

   Answer _____

4. The perimeter of a rectangular patio is 60 feet. Find the length if the width is 10 feet.

   Answer _____

5. Mr. Callahan bought a roll of fencing 360 feet long to enclose a pen. If he uses all the fencing and makes the rectangular pen 120 feet long, how wide will the pen be?

   Answer _____

6. Mrs. Gates makes place mats to sell at craft fairs. If each place mat is 18 inches long and she is able to trim each one using exactly 5 feet of decorative binding, how wide is each place mat? (Hint: Change feet to inches.)

   Answer _____

Using the Area Formula

The formula for finding the area of a rectangle, $A = lw$, can also be used to find the length of one side if the total area and the length of the other side are given. To find the length of the unknown side, divide the area by the known side.

The area of a rectangle is 48 square inches. Find the width if the length is 8 inches.

Substitute.

$A = lw$
$48 = 8w$

Divide.

$\dfrac{48}{8} = \dfrac{8w}{8}$
$6 = w$

$l = 8$ in.

Solve.

1. The area of a rectangle is 200 square feet. Find the length if the width is 10 feet.
   $A = lw$
   $200 = 10l$
   $\dfrac{200}{10} = \dfrac{10l}{10}$
   $20 = l$

   Answer _____20 feet_____

2. The area of a rectangle is 350 square meters. Find the length if the width is 70 meters.

   Answer _____

3. The area of a playroom in a day-care center is 600 square feet. Find the width if the length is 30 feet.

   Answer _____

4. The area of a dog run at a kennel is 300 square meters. Find the length if the width is 10 meters.

   Answer _____

5. An acre is 43,560 square feet. Find the width if the length is 660 feet.

   Answer _____

6. What is the length of a 14,520-square foot vacant lot if the width of the lot is 120 feet?

   Answer _____

35

Using the Volume Formula

The formula for finding the volume of a rectangular solid, $V = lwh$, can also be used to find the length of the third side when the length of the other two sides and the volume are given. To find the length of the unknown side, divide the volume by the product of the two known sides.

The volume of a rectangular solid is 216 cubic centimeters. Find the height if the length is 9 centimeters and the width is 4 centimeters.

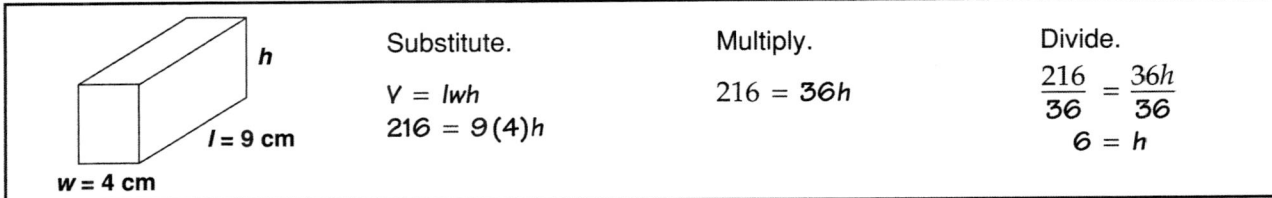

Substitute.
$V = lwh$
$216 = 9(4)h$

Multiply.
$216 = 36h$

Divide.
$\dfrac{216}{36} = \dfrac{36h}{36}$
$6 = h$

Solve.

1. The volume of a rectangular solid is 24 cubic inches. Find the width if the length is 2 inches and the height is 3 inches.
   $V = lwh$
   $24 = 2(w)3$
   $24 = 6w$
   $\dfrac{24}{6} = \dfrac{6w}{6}$
   $4 = w$

   Answer _____ 4 inches _____

2. The volume of a rectangular solid is 12 cubic feet. Find the length of the solid if the width is 2 feet and height is 1 foot.

   Answer _____

3. A packing crate has a volume of 7,776 cubic inches. If the height is 18 inches and the width is 18 inches, what is the length?

   Answer _____

4. A form for making concrete blocks has a volume of 288 cubic inches. If the form is 12 inches on each side, what is the height?

   Answer _____

5. The Petersons bought a sandbox for their children. Find the height of the sandbox if the volume is 80 cubic feet, the length is 8 feet, and the width is 5 feet.

   Answer _____

6. A storage trunk has a volume of 48 cubic feet. Find the width of the trunk if the length is 6 feet and the height is 2 feet.

   Answer _____

Using the Pythagorean Theorem

The Pythagorean Theorem shows the relationship of the lengths of the sides of a right triangle to each other. This equation shows that the sum of the squares of the two shorter sides (the legs) equals the square of the third side (the hypotenuse). The hypotenuse is always opposite the right angle. Use this formula to find any one side when you know the other two.

The length of the hypotenuse of a right triangle is 5 feet. The length of one leg is 3 feet. What is the length of the other leg?

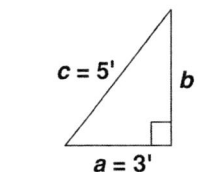

Substitute.

$a^2 + b^2 = c^2$
$3^2 + b^2 = 5^2$

Square the sides given.

$9 + b^2 = 25$

Subtract and find the square root.

$9 - 9 + b^2 = 25 - 9$
$b^2 = 16$
$b = \sqrt{16} = 4$

Find the unknown side in each right triangle.

1. The length of the hypotenuse is 13 inches. The length of one leg is 5 inches. What is the length of the other leg?

    $a^2 + b^2 = c^2$
    $5^2 + b^2 = 13^2$
    $25 + b^2 = 169$
    $25 - 25 + b^2 = 169 - 25$
    $b^2 = 144$
    $b = \sqrt{144} = 12$

    Answer _____12 inches_____

2. A 20-foot ladder is placed against the side of a house. The bottom of the ladder is 12 feet from the house. How high up will the ladder reach on the wall?

    Answer _____

3. Marco drives 18 miles south, turns east, and then drives 24 miles to get from his pet shop to his house. If a new road is built in a straight line from Marco's shop to his house, how long will the new road be? (Hint: Draw a right triangle with the information given.)

    Answer _____

4. The community van service travels on a 40-mile route west from the airport to downtown. From downtown, the bus goes 30 miles north to the city bus station at Cortland. What is the length of the direct bus trip directly from Cortland back to the airport? (Hint: Draw a picture of the van's route.)

    Answer _____

Ratios

A ratio is a fraction that shows a relationship between two numbers. For example, if there are 12 supervisors in a company and 240 employees, the ratio of supervisors to employees is 12 to 240 or $\frac{12}{240}$ or $\frac{1}{20}$. Ratios may be reduced without changing the relationship. A ratio is always written as a fraction even if the denominator is 1.

Write a ratio to show 12 cups of water to 2 cups of cleaning solution.

Write the first number as the numerator of the fraction. $\underline{12}$	Write the second number as the denominator. $\frac{12}{2}$	Reduce the fraction. $\frac{12}{2} = \frac{6}{1}$

Write a ratio for each problem. Reduce if possible.

1. 3 pizzas for 6 people   4 hits out of 10 times at bat   3 teachers for 45 children
   $\frac{3}{6} = \frac{1}{2}$

2. 8 yards of material for 3 dresses   7 feet to 2 feet   3 cans of beans for $1.00

3. 15 problems correct out of 20   4 out of 5 doctors   3 waiters for 30 customers

4. 24 miles to 1 gallon of gas $20 for 4 children   5 doctors for 125 patients

5. 3 pounds of chicken for 9 people   7 wins and 7 losses   2 bedrooms for 4 children

6. 5 hours for 3 games   60 pencils for 30 students   275 miles in 5 hours

Solve.

7. Jane received $ .90 for recycling 3 pounds of aluminum cans. Write the ratio of money received to the pounds of cans recycled.

   Answer _____

8. Kevin pays $100 property tax on his house valued at $50,000. Write the ratio of tax paid to the value of the house.

   Answer _____

Proportions

Equal ratios are called proportions. Proportions are used to solve equations when the relationship between two amounts is known. For example, if Mina can make 3 telephone sales calls in 10 minutes, how many calls can she make in 30 minutes?

Find n. $\dfrac{3}{10} = \dfrac{n}{30}$

Cross-multiply.	Divide each side by the number next to n.	Check by substituting 3 for n and cross-multiplying.
$\dfrac{3}{10} = \dfrac{n}{30}$ $n \times 10 = 3 \times 30$ $10n = 90$	$\dfrac{10n}{10} = \dfrac{90}{10}$ $n = 9$	$\dfrac{3}{10} = \dfrac{9}{30}$ $9 \times 10 = 3 \times 30$ $90 = 90$

Find n. Check your answers.

1. $\dfrac{n}{6} = \dfrac{3}{2}$ $\qquad$ $\dfrac{2}{n} = \dfrac{4}{8}$ $\qquad$ $\dfrac{8}{12} = \dfrac{n}{3}$ $\qquad$ $\dfrac{5}{9} = \dfrac{15}{n}$
   $n \times 2 = 3 \times 6$
   $\dfrac{2n}{2} = \dfrac{18}{2}$
   $n = 9$

2. $\dfrac{7}{8} = \dfrac{n}{16}$ $\qquad$ $\dfrac{n}{10} = \dfrac{15}{50}$ $\qquad$ $\dfrac{13}{n} = \dfrac{39}{42}$ $\qquad$ $\dfrac{42}{60} = \dfrac{7}{n}$

3. $\dfrac{n}{18} = \dfrac{3}{6}$ $\qquad$ $\dfrac{21}{n} = \dfrac{3}{7}$ $\qquad$ $\dfrac{1}{16} = \dfrac{n}{48}$ $\qquad$ $\dfrac{34}{36} = \dfrac{17}{n}$

4. $\dfrac{2}{n} = \dfrac{22}{33}$ $\qquad$ $\dfrac{2}{10} = \dfrac{n}{5}$ $\qquad$ $\dfrac{4}{8} = \dfrac{1}{n}$ $\qquad$ $\dfrac{n}{14} = \dfrac{6}{42}$

5. $\dfrac{25}{n} = \dfrac{50}{100}$ $\qquad$ $\dfrac{n}{9} = \dfrac{1}{3}$ $\qquad$ $\dfrac{1}{8} = \dfrac{n}{24}$ $\qquad$ $\dfrac{12}{60} = \dfrac{2}{n}$

Solve.

6. One store sells 2 pairs of socks for $3. How much will 4 pairs of socks cost?

   Answer _____

7. Ernest can type 165 words in 3 minutes without errors. At that rate, how many words can Ernest type in 1 minute?

   Answer _____

Similar Triangles

Proportions can be used to find the length of an unknown side in a set of similar triangles. If triangle ABC is similar to (~) triangle XYZ, then the corresponding sides form proportions $\frac{AB}{XY} = \frac{AC}{XZ} = \frac{BC}{YZ}$.

Triangle ABC is similar to triangle XYZ. If $\overline{AC}$ = 6 inches, $\overline{XZ}$ = 3 inches, and $\overline{YZ}$ = 4 inches, what is the length of $\overline{BC}$?

Write a proportion. Substitute.	Cross-multiply.	Divide.
$\frac{AC}{XZ} = \frac{BC}{YZ}$ $\frac{6}{3} = \frac{n}{4}$	$6 \times 4 = n \times 3$ $24 = 3n$	$\frac{24}{3} = \frac{3n}{3}$ $8 = n$

Solve.

1. Triangle ABC is similar to triangle DEF. Find the length of $\overline{DF}$.

   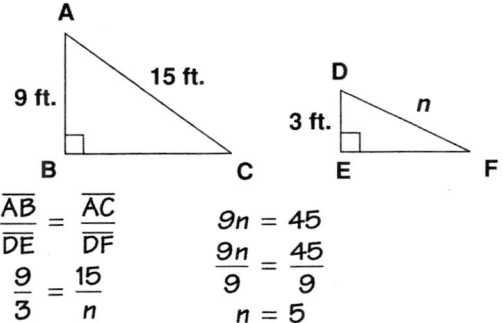

   $\frac{AB}{DE} = \frac{AC}{DF}$ $9n = 45$
   $\frac{9}{3} = \frac{15}{n}$ $\frac{9n}{9} = \frac{45}{9}$
   $n = 5$

   Answer _____ $\overline{DF}$ = 5 ft. _____

2. Triangle LMN is similar to triangle RST. Find the length of $\overline{LM}$.

   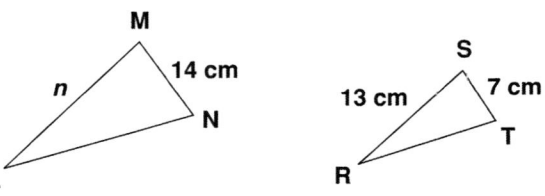

   Answer _____

3. Use the drawing to find the height of the flagpole.

   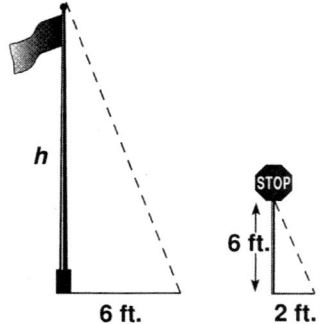

   Answer _____

4. Use the drawing to find the distance across the pond. Use d for the distance.

   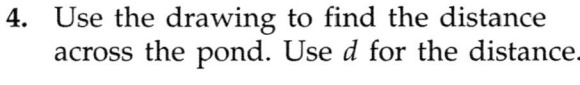
   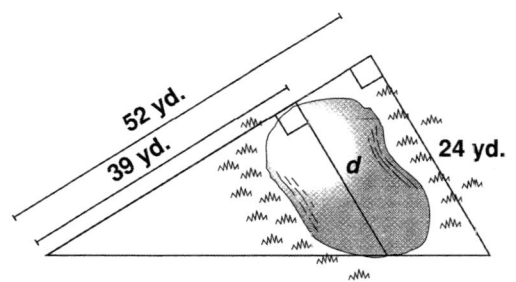

   Answer _____

Checking Up

Solve.

1. The perimeter of a rectangular deck is 120 feet. If the width is 20 feet, what is the length?

   Answer _____

2. City Hospital bought 25 new television sets at a cost of $375 per set to put in the wards for patients. What was the total cost of the television sets?

   Answer _____

3. The area of Greg's yard is 3,000 square feet. If the length of the yard is 100 feet, what is the width?

   Answer _____

4. After 1 year, Jennifer paid $25 in simple interest on a loan. If she paid an annual interest rate of 5%, what was the amount of the loan?

   Answer _____

5. A storage box has a volume of 12 cubic feet. If the height is 2 feet and the length is 6 feet, what is the width?

   Answer _____

6. If a parade travels at a rate of 10 miles per hour, how long will it take for the parade to travel the 5-mile parade route?

   Answer _____

7. Use the drawing to find the height of the taller tree.

   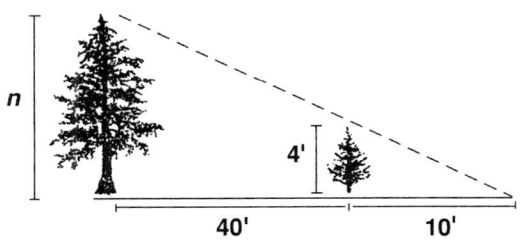

   Answer _____

8. The walking path down the middle of the part of the city park shown in the drawing divides the large triangle into two right triangles. What is the length of the walking path?

   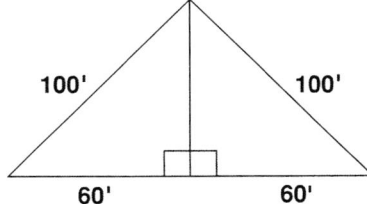

   Answer _____

41

Graphing an Equation

You can graph solutions to equations with two variables. An example is $y = x + 1$. This equation has many solutions. These solutions, called ordered pairs (x,y), form a straight line on the coordinate graph.

To find one solution, or ordered pair, choose a value for x and solve for y.

$x = 1 \quad y = x + 1$
$\quad\quad\quad\; y = 1 + 1 = 2$

The ordered pair is (1,2). The point is plotted on the graph. Then find another ordered pair and plot that point on the graph.

$x = -2 \quad y = x + 1$
$\quad\quad\quad\;\; y = -2 + 1 = -1$

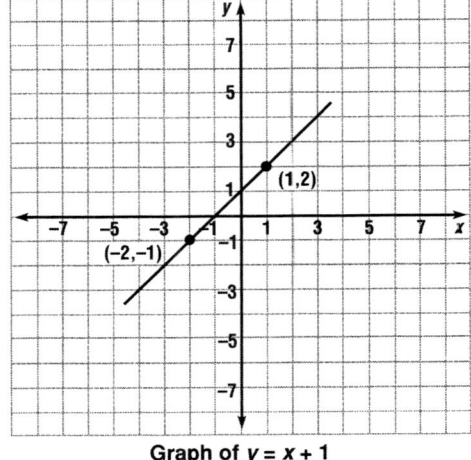

Graph of $y = x + 1$

The ordered pair is (−2,−1). When the point is plotted on the graph, a straight line can be drawn connecting the points. This is the graph of $y = x + 1$. If you find other solutions for this equation and plot them on the graph, you will see that they are also points along the same straight line.

1. Find two points on the line $y = -x + 2$. Plot the points and draw the line.

   $x = -2 \quad y = -x + 2$
   $\quad\quad\quad\;\; y = -(-2) + 2$
   $\quad\quad\quad\;\; y = 4$

   $x = 2 \quad\; y = -x + 2$
   $\quad\quad\quad\;\; y = -2 + 2$
   $\quad\quad\quad\;\; y = 0$

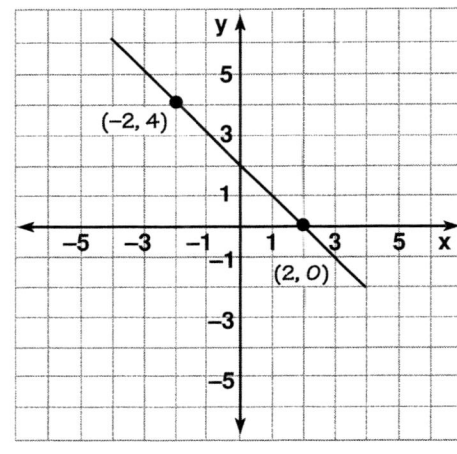

2. Find two points on the line $y = \frac{1}{2}x - 1$. Plot the points and draw the line. (Use 2 and 4 for the values of x.)

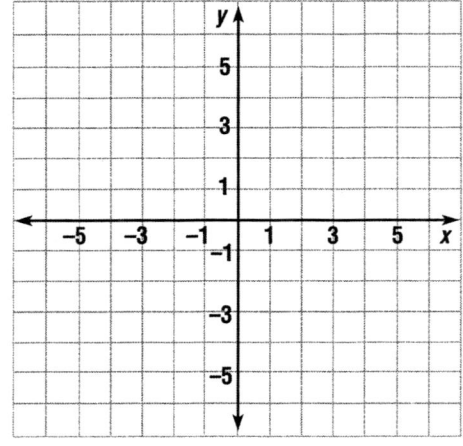

3. Find two points on the line $y = 2x - 3$. Plot the points and draw the line. (Use 0 and 3 for the values of x.)

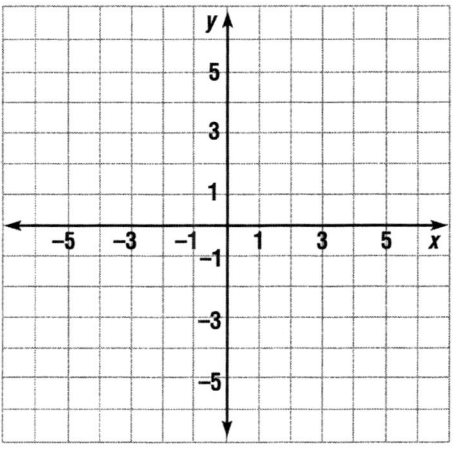

Slope of a Line

The slope of a line is a number that tells you how steep the line is and which way it slants. All lines that go up as they move from left to right have a positive slope. All lines that go down as they move from left to right have a negative slope.

To find the slope (m) of a line, use any two points on the line, (x_1, y_1) and (x_2, y_2). Substitute the values of the coordinates into the formula.

$$m = \frac{y_2 - y_1}{x_2 - x_1}$$

Use (–2, –4) and (2, 0).

$$m = \frac{0 - (-4)}{2 - (-2)}$$

$$m = \frac{4}{4} = 1$$

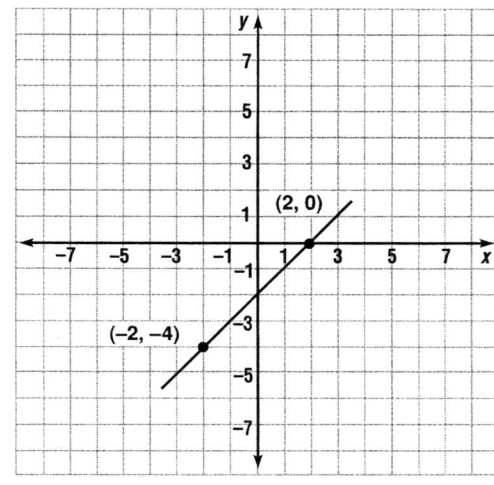

Find the slope of each line.

1.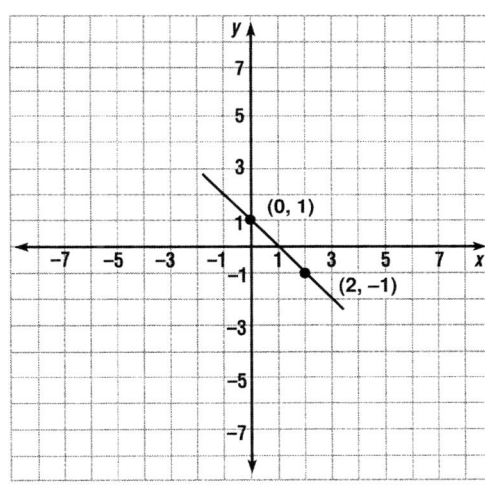

$$m = \frac{1 - (-1)}{0 - 2}$$

$$m = \frac{2}{-2} = -1$$

2.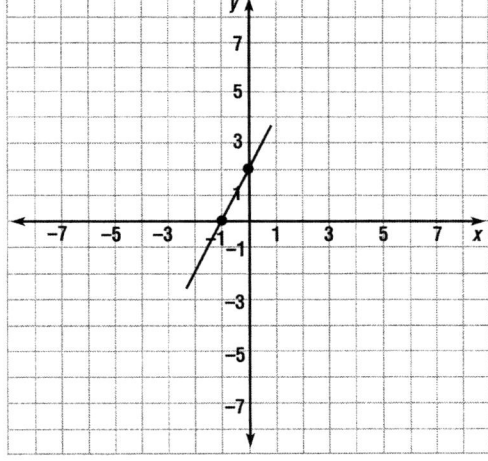

3.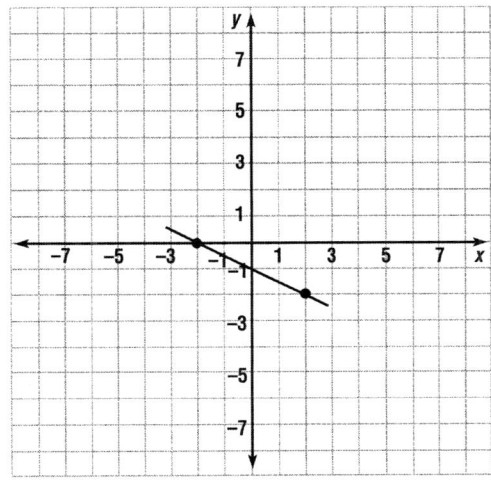

4.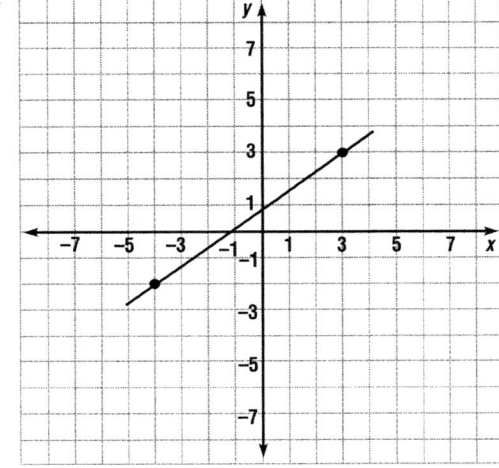

Progress Review

Compare. Write < or >.

1. $-3 \square -4$ $9 \square -9$ $-12 \square -11$ $0 \square -6$

Evaluate each expression.

2. $2^2 \times (4 + 6)$ $13 + 2 \div (5 - \sqrt{9})$ $7^2 + 8^2 \div 2 + 6$

Evaluate each expression if $x = 6$ and $y = 4$.

3. $x^2 \cdot (4 - y)$ $2y - \dfrac{x}{3}$ $x^2 + y^2$ $\dfrac{4x}{y} \div x$

Add, subtract, multiply, or divide.

4. $6 + (-3)$ $12 - (-9)$ $\dfrac{-15}{-3}$ $-7(-8)$

5. $\dfrac{-45}{9} + 15$ $81 + (9)(-9)$ $4(-6) - 9$ $\dfrac{64}{-4} - (-6)(9)$

6. $(-2)(-12)(-5)$ $16 + (-8) - (-4)$ $\dfrac{100}{5} - 3(2)$ $37 - (-8)$

Solve each equation.

7. $y - 3 = 12$ $-5x = 15$ $\dfrac{x}{8} = -2$ $9 + x = 16$

8. $\dfrac{3x}{5} = -30$ $\dfrac{8}{y} = -4$ $x - 6 = 10$ $y + 9 = 9$

9. $3x - 1 = 5$ $\dfrac{2y}{3} = -8$ $\dfrac{1}{2}x - 6 = 10$ $4 - 3y = 25$

Solve for y if $x = 9$.

10. $y + x = 10$ $y = x - 3$ $x = y + 8$ $x - 2y = 5$

Solve each proportion.

11. $\dfrac{n}{3} = \dfrac{2}{6}$ $\dfrac{8}{n} = \dfrac{2}{3}$ $\dfrac{1}{6} = \dfrac{n}{18}$ $\dfrac{10}{25} = \dfrac{2}{n}$

Solve.

12. Potatoes are on sale 8 pounds for $2. Write the ratio of the number of pounds to the cost.

Answer _____

13. How many pounds of potatoes can you buy for $5 if 8 pounds are $2?

Answer _____

14. The area of a garden is 96 square yards. If the length is 12 yards, what is the width?

Answer _____

15. An auto supply store sells a case of oil for $21.60. If there are 24 cans of oil in a case, how much is one can of oil?

Answer _____

16. How much interest will you earn in 6 months if you deposit $200 in a savings account that earns $5\frac{1}{4}\%$ interest annually?

Answer _____

17. The volume of a box is 4 cubic feet. If the width is 1 foot and the length is 2 feet, what is the height?

Answer _____

18. The perimeter of a rectangle is 80 inches. If the width is 15 inches, what is the length?

Answer _____

19. The speed limit on a road under construction is 45 miles per hour. How far will a car travel on that road in 3 hours at that rate?

Answer _____

20. The hypotenuse of a right triangle is 39 centimeters long. If one leg is 15 centimeters, what is the length of the other leg?

Answer _____

21. Triangle ABC is similar to triangle XYZ. Find the length of $\overline{AC}$.

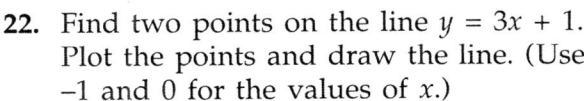

Answer _____

22. Find two points on the line $y = 3x + 1$. Plot the points and draw the line. (Use −1 and 0 for the values of x.)

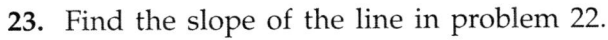

23. Find the slope of the line in problem 22.

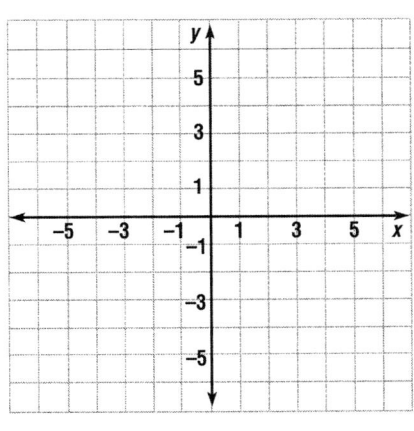

ANSWER KEY

Page 2
1. A G F J O
2. E H K N C
3. I L B M D
4. −13 1 5 −20 −10
5. 19 13 4 −1 −17
6. 9 17 10 −4 −6
7. 5 −7 0
8. 4 −6 10
9. 4 −5 3
10. 0 1 −11

Page 3
1. −2 < 3   4 > −3   0 < 2
   −6 < −5   12 > −12
2. −5 > −10   1 > −2   −15 < 5
   −19 < 9   10 > 3
3. 17 > 12   −8 < −7   −6 < 0
   14 > −13   7 > −7
4. −3 < 2   16 > 12   −4 < 4
   −8 > −9   −11 < 10
5. −14 > −15   −20 < −16   −17 < 17
   −1 > −2   3 > 0
6. 5 > −10   6 < 8   −12 < 10
   15 > −1   19 > −19
7. −10 < −4   8 > −8   −7 < 6
   3 > 1   −16 < −13
8. 11 < 12   20 > −16   −18 < −17
   13 > 0   −20 < −5
9. −10, 0, 3   −7, 7, 9
   −12, −4, 2   −15, −8, −6
10. 0, 8, 15   −11, −2, 16
    −20, 5, 14   −1, 0, 2
11. −18, −16, −13   −14, 6, 20
    −3, −2, 1   −8, −5, 9
12. −20°
13. 3,000 feet
14. 3°
15. −1,000 feet

Page 4
1. 9 8 64 49 2
2. 10 729 216 196 144
3. 512 6 25 4 1
4. 1,000 12 4,096 125 36
5. 13 64 8 81 11
6. 5 400 0 16 7
7. 256 square feet
8. 8 cubic feet

Page 5
1. 34 1 20 12
2. 24 98 63 20
3. 11 40 5 12
4. 5 23 11 11
5. 9 1 17 6
6. 0 0 3 11
7. 81 10 26 4
8. 72 7 57 2

Page 6
1. 121 30 1
2. 16 94 3
3. 98 41 34
4. 10 200 17
5. 180 60 3
6. 130 15 1
7. 5 12 20
8. 13 20 38
9. 22 63 2
10. 1 56 10

Page 7
1. $3 \cdot 17 = 51$ $5 + 7 − 4 = 8$
2. $8 \div 2 \cdot 2 = 8$ $13 − 7 = 6$
3. $5^2 + 9 = 34$ $100 + 60 + 4 = 164$
4. $85 \div 5 = 17$ $27 + 3 − 15 = 15$
5. $42 \div 7 = 6$ $30 \cdot 3 \div 10 = 9$
6. $(13 + 17) \div 10 = 3$
7. $(15 − 9) \cdot 6 = 36$
8. $(14.00 + 3.80 + 2.20) \div 4 = \$5.00$
9. $3(12 − 9) + 4(6 − 1) + (12 − 9) = 32$ hours

Page 8
1. c
2. d
3. a
4. b
5. $6x$ $x + 3$
6. $8x$ $15 \div x$ or $\frac{15}{x}$
7. $11 + x$ $x − 12$
8. $5 \cdot 7 \cdot x$ $24 − x + 6$
9. $32 \div x$ or $\frac{32}{x}$ $\frac{x}{7}$
10. $50 \cdot x \div 3$ $4 + x − 2$
11. $(8 + x) \div 3$
12. $(30 − x) \cdot 7$

Page 9
1. 13 22 2 9
2. 31 36 6 24
3. 40 14 40 1
4. 15 10 22 318
5. 4 36 17 4
6. 8 1 7 40
7. 10 1 48 100
8. 30 3 6 39

Page 10
1. 13 34 2 16
2. 7 51 21 2
3. 20 80 12 84
4. 16 1 12 8
5. 35 6 45 250
6. 80 40 75 5
7. 12 56 44 2
8. 9 206 16 15

Page 11
1. $x = 4$ $y = 8$
   $p = 3$ $n = 1$
2. $a = 12$ $q = 3$
   $z = 2$ $r = 0$
3. $x = 3$ $b = 12$
   $y = 1$ $t = 5$
4. $p = 8$ $a = 8$
   $n = 4$ $x = 4$
5. $q = 6$ $x = 9$
   $y = 8$ $r = 4$
6. $n = 3$ $p = 9$
   $b = 4$ $m = 20$
7. $t = 6$ $x = 9$
   $r = 7$ $n = 42$
8. $p = 9$ $q = 9$
   $x = 8$ $y = 14$
9. $m = 7$ $n = 9$
   $x = 17$ $y = 7$

Page 12
1. $y = 1$ $y = 6$
   $y = 1$ $y = 25$
2. $y = 35$ $y = 4$
   $y = 3$ $y = 4$
3. $x = 14$ $x = 5$
   $x = 50$ $x = 7$
4. $x = 30$ $x = 13$
   $x = 90$ $x = 10$
5. $b = 2$ $b = 1$
   $b = 8$ $b = 12$
6. $b = 2$ $b = 16$
   $b = 81$ $b = 3$
7. $a = 24$ $a = 4$
   $a = 5$ $a = 1$
8. $a = 6$ $a = 72$
   $a = 1$ $a = 8$

Page 13
1. −12 < −11   0 > −9   7 > −7
   2 < 12   −4 > −10
2. −7, −5, 0   −8, 0, 6
   −6, −4, −1   −1, 1, 3
3. $7 − 3$ $25 + 6 − 12$
4. $4b$ $\frac{80}{b}$
5. 4 5 28
6. 69 1 5 3
7. $x = 4$ $y = 5$
   $b = 5$ $n = 2$
8. $y = 3$ $y = 2$
   $y = 12$ $y = 5$
9. 119 miles
10. 10 flowers

Page 14
1. −17 −9 15 −29
2. −14 −27 −5 −16
3. 0 5 −7 −3
4. −8 12 16 −24
5. 12 −18 0 −8
6. −22 −10 −39 10
7. −5 0 9 −9
8. −7 −10 −28 −4
9. 16 −14 −16 −19
10. −38 −3 0 −10

Page 15
1. −16 −1 17 −8
2. −7 −20 26 12
3. 3 0 14 2
4. −18 0 24 −15
5. 11 27 21 4
6. 5 −4 −24 7
7. 12 −45 −15 40
8. 25 −17 23 0
9. 3 10 −4 −12
10. 22 −20 −39 −15
11. −27 −21 −24 0
12. 17 −17 −19 −9
13. −25 −4 28 0

Page 16
1. 3 4 −25
2. −31 12 0
3. 4 22 4
4. 16 −24 −26
5. −6 −12 −25
6. −20 −2 −33
7. 20 −17 −44
8. −12 14 0
9. −9 −17 7
10. 5 −2 4

Page 17
1. $x = 7$ $x = -14$
   $x = -16$ $x = 3$
2. $x = -12$ $x = 5$
   $x = -4$ $x = 20$
3. $x = -23$ $x = -3$
   $x = 15$ $x = -5$
4. $x = 7$ $x = -10$
   $x = -3$ $x = -14$
5. $x = -8$ $x = 14$
   $x = -30$ $x = -44$
6. $x = -25$ $x = -34$
   $x = -23$ $x = 39$
7. $x = -6$ $x = -21$
   $x = 1$ $x = -28$
8. $x = -14$ $x = 17$
   $x = -13$ $x = -60$
9. $x = -44$ $x = 14$
   $x = -12$ $x = 12$

Page 18
1. $x = 5$ $x = -1$
   $x = 18$ $x = 2$
2. $x = 6$ $x = 6$
   $x = -7$ $x = 11$
3. $x = 9$ $x = -5$
   $x = 9$ $x = 19$
4. $x = 7$ $x = 14$
   $x = -5$ $x = 6$
5. $x = -3$ $x = -6$
   $x = 39$ $x = 1$
6. $x = 17$ $x = 18$
   $x = 11$ $x = -2$
7. $x = -4$ $x = 52$
   $x = -33$ $x = 60$
8. $x = 82$ $x = -18$
   $x = 60$ $x = -6$
9. $x = 6$ $x = 38$
   $x = 67$ $x = -20$

Page 19
1. −15   0   16   25
2. −12   3   2   −23
3. 8   −20   −8   5
4. −15   −18   −8   19
5. −29   −3   8   −1
6. −32   −48   18   −27
7. $x = 5$ $x = -7$
   $x = 9$ $x = 18$
8. $x = -7$ $x = -5$
   $x = -16$ $x = 0$
9. $x = -4$ $x = -25$
   $x = 8$ $x = -6$
10. $x = 21$ $x = 6$
    $x = 2$ $x = 12$
11. $x = -8$ $x = 6$
    $x = -2$ $x = 7$
12. $x = -18$ $x = -8$
    $x = 12$ $x = 37$

Page 20
1. −27   30   −32   −72
2. 5   −14   −108   −22
3. 2   12   −42   110
4. 108   −150   120   −48
5. −48   −81   77   −22
6. −54   182   −45
7. 80   42   600
8. 0   −162   −42
9. 192   −336   216

Page 21
1. −4   7   −2   −5
2. 7   −6   −8   10
3. 6   −4   −9   −8
4. 4   −4   −1   10
5. −2   −9   −4   3
6. 5   −8   −4   −7
7. 3   −9   −3   −2
8. 11   1   −2   −3
9. 3   −2   2   1
10. −4   −10   8   −11
11. 2   −25   −7   19

Page 22
1. −1   9   −40   −15
2. 0   −18   −4   72
3. −5   −52   −15   −2
4. −96   6   31   −11
5. 3   0   −54   −5
6. 60   −4   −13   −13
7. −11   270   23   −9
8. −5   −55   −128   −16
9. −13   −24   −6   113
10. 0   −8   3   −4
11. −74   10   37   −20
12. −15   0   12   −107
13. 9   −54   200   0

Page 23
1. $x = -4$ $x = 4$
   $x = 4$ $x = -2$
2. $x = 2$ $x = -3$
   $x = -6$ $x = -7$
3. $x = 5$ $x = 6$
   $x = -8$ $x = 3$
4. $x = -3$ $x = -6$
   $x = -3$ $x = -2$
5. $x = 6$ $x = -5$
   $x = 3$ $x = -9$
6. $x = 7$ $x = -1$
   $x = 0$ $x = -6$
7. $x = -2$ $x = -3$
   $x = 3$ $x = 4$
8. $x = -3$ $x = -10$
   $x = 2$ $x = 8$
9. $x = -1$ $x = 9$
   $x = -8$ $x = -5$

Page 24
1. $x = -30$ $x = 32$
   $x = 36$ $x = 18$
2. $x = 80$ $x = 28$
   $x = -75$ $x = -56$
3. $x = -36$ $x = -18$
   $x = 120$ $x = 60$
4. $x = 3$ $x = -10$
   $x = -24$ $x = 15$
5. $x = -140$ $x = -56$
   $x = 80$ $x = 45$
6. $x = 14$ $x = -9$
   $x = 72$ $x = 24$
7. $x = 44$ $x = 10$
   $x = 48$ $x = -55$
8. $x = 45$ $x = 117$
   $x = 54$ $x = 48$
9. $x = -25$ $x = 49$
   $x = 80$ $x = -36$

Page 25
1. −8   27   −8   −60
2. −5   50   −130   −18
3. −56   6   288   6
4. −8   −42   4   0
5. 13   15   −12   −9
6. 5   −10   29   −8
7. −9   0   −33   −35
8. −32   30   −4   −4
9. $x = 0$ $x = -9$
   $x = 7$ $x = -27$
10. $x = -3$ $x = -35$
    $x = 24$ $x = 34$
11. $x = -1$ $x = 51$
    $x = -68$ $x = 4$
12. $x = -30$ $x = -1$
    $x = -7$ $x = -48$
13. $x = -20$ $x = -63$
    $x = 33$ $x = 2$
14. $x = 17$ $x = -4$
    $x = 30$ $x = 32$

Page 26
1. $y = -24$ $x = -9$ $x = -25$
2. $y = -36$ $x = 24$ $x = -42$
3. $y = -9$ $y = 20$ $y = 24$
4. $x = 33$ $x = -39$ $x = -30$
5. $y = 60$ $y = -15$ $x = 90$

Page 27
1. $x = 2$ $x = 24$ $x = 12$
2. $x = 7$ $y = -1$ $y = 5$
3. $y = 8$ $x = -9$ $y = 45$
4. $x = -1$ $y = -8$ $y = -7$
5. $y = 1$ $x = 2$ $y = 3$

Page 28
1. $x = -12$ $x = 3$ $x = -6$
2. $x = 28$ $x = -2$ $x = 2$
3. $x = -20$ $x = -4$ $x = 8$
4. $x = -12$ $x = -7$ $x = -2$
5. $x = -6$ $x = 5$ $x = -18$

Page 29
1. $x = 27$ $y = -9$ $x = -21$
2. $x = -10$ $y = 20$ $y = -8$
3. $y = 20$ $x = 1$ $x = 3$
4. $x = 3$ $y = 1$ $y = 40$
5. $x = 10$ $y = 2$ $x = 90$
6. $x = -12$ $x = -6$ $y = 27$
7. $x = 4$ $y = -3$ $x = 8$
8. $y = -30$ $x = -11$ $y = 12$

Page 30
1. 6 hours
2. 50 mph
3. 3 hours
4. 390 miles
5. 600 mph
6. 7.5 miles

Page 31
1. 4%
2. $1,000
3. $3,000
4. $200
5. 20%
6. 2 years

Page 32
1. $125
2. $ .25
3. 24
4. $4.50
5. $7.50
6. 50

47

Page 33
1. c   225 miles
2. b $1,000
3. b $10.80
4. a   10 miles
5. b $33.75
6. c $182
7. a   20 mph
8. b   20 years

Page 34
1. 10 feet
2. 13 centimeters
3. 15 feet
4. 20 feet
5. 60 feet
6. 12 inches

Page 35
1. 20 feet
2. 5 meters
3. 20 feet
4. 30 meters
5. 66 feet
6. 121 feet

Page 36
1. 4 inches
2. 6 feet
3. 24 inches
4. 2 inches
5. 2 feet
6. 4 feet

Page 37
1. 12 inches
2. 16 feet
3. 30 miles
4. 50 miles

Page 38
1. $\frac{1}{2}$ $\frac{2}{5}$ $\frac{1}{15}$
2. $\frac{8}{3}$ $\frac{7}{2}$ $\frac{3}{1}$
3. $\frac{3}{4}$ $\frac{4}{5}$ $\frac{1}{10}$
4. $\frac{24}{1}$ $\frac{5}{1}$ $\frac{1}{25}$
5. $\frac{1}{3}$ $\frac{1}{1}$ $\frac{1}{2}$
6. $\frac{5}{3}$ $\frac{2}{1}$ $\frac{55}{1}$
7. $\frac{.30}{1}$
8. $\frac{1}{500}$

Page 39
1. $n = 9$ $n = 4$
    $n = 2$ $n = 27$
2. $n = 14$ $n = 3$
    $n = 14$ $n = 10$
3. $n = 9$ $n = 49$
    $n = 3$ $n = 18$
4. $n = 3$ $n = 1$
    $n = 2$ $n = 2$
5. $n = 50$ $n = 3$
    $n = 3$ $n = 10$

Page 40
1. $\overline{DF} = 5$ ft.
2. $\overline{LM} = 26$ cm
3. $h = 18$ ft.
4. $d = 18$ yd.

Page 41
1. 40 feet
2. $9,375
3. 30 feet
4. $500
5. 1 foot
6. $\frac{1}{2}$ hour
7. $n = 20'$
8. 80'

Page 42
1. (−2,4), (2,0)
2. (2,0), (4,1)

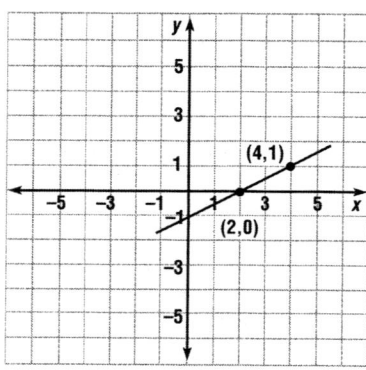

3. (0,−3), (3,3)

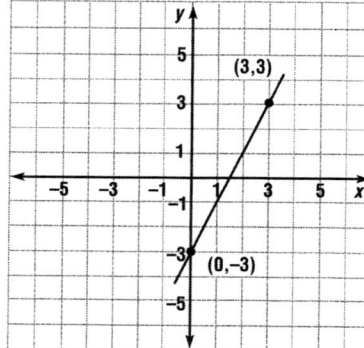

Page 43
1. $m = -1$
2. $m = 2$
3. $m = \frac{-1}{2}$
4. $m = \frac{5}{7}$

Page 44
1. −3 > −4   9 > −9
    −12 < −11   0 > −6
2. 40   14   87
3. 0   6   52   1
4. 3   21   5   56
5. 10   0   −33   38
6. −120   12   14   45

7. $y = 15$ $x = -3$
    $x = -16$ $x = 7$
8. $x = -50$ $y = -2$
    $x = 16$ $y = 0$
9. $x = 2$ $y = -12$
    $x = 32$ $y = -7$
10. $y = 1$ $y = 6$
     $y = 1$ $y = 2$
11. $n = 1$ $n = 12$
     $n = 3$ $n = 5$

Page 45
12. $\frac{4}{1}$
13. 20 pounds
14. 8 yards
15. $ .90
16. $5.25
17. 2 feet
18. 25 inches
19. 135 miles
20. 36 centimeters
21. 20
22. (−1,−2), (0,1)

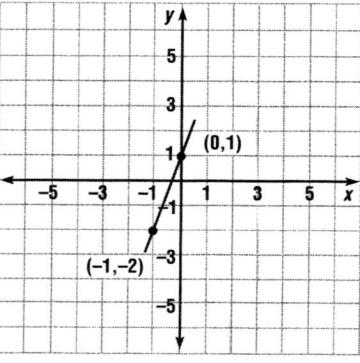

23. $m = 3$